Digital Copyright
Second edition

Paul Pedley

facet publishing

© Paul Pedley 2005, 2007

Published by Facet Publishing
7 Ridgmount Street, London WC1E 7AE
www.facetpublishing.co.uk

Facet Publishing is wholly owned by CILIP: the Chartered Institute of Library and
Information Professionals.

British Library Cataloguing in Publication Data
A catalogue record for this book is available from the British Library.

ISBN 978-1-85604-608-4

First published as an e-book 2005
This second edition 2007

Typeset from author's disk in 11/15 pt Aldine and Myriad by Facet Publishing.
Printed and made in Great Britain by Cromwell Press Ltd, Trowbridge, Wiltshire.

Contents

Acknowledgements and information

The author would like to express his gratitude to Graham Cornish of Copyright Circle for reading the text and offering comments and feedback.

The pre-digitization checklist on page 129 is reproduced with the kind permission of Alan Rae.

Biographical note

Paul Pedley MA MLib FCLIP is Head of Research at the Economist Intelligence Unit. He is a member of the Libraries and Archives Copyright Alliance, CILIP's Freedom of Information Panel and the Information Rights Forum. Also Visiting Professor at London Metropolitan University, and editor of the *Keeping Within the Law* subscription service (Facet Publishing, www.kwtl.co.uk), Paul regularly runs training courses on copyright and other legal issues.

Disclaimer

Paul Pedley is not a lawyer and is not able to give legal advice.

Copyright notice

Abbreviations

AAP	American Association of Publishers
ABPI	Association of the British Pharmaceutical Industry
ALCS	Authors' Licensing and Collecting Society
ALPSP	Association of Learned and Professional Society Publishers
APPSI	Advisory Panel on Public Sector Information
BBC	British Broadcasting Corporation
BHB	British Horseracing Board
BPI	British Phonographic Industry
CCC	Copyright Clearance Center
CDPA	Copyright Designs and Patents Act 1988
CD-ROM	Compact Disc – Read Only Memory
CILIP	Chartered Institute of Library and Information Professionals
CLA	Copyright Licensing Agency
DACS	Design and Artists Copyright Society
DIUS	Department for Innovation, Universities and Skills
DRM	Digital Rights Management
DTI	Department of Trade and Industry
DVD	Digital Versatile Discs
ECMS	Electronic Copyright Management Systems
ECUP	European Copyright User Platform
FE	Further Education
HE	Higher Education
HMRC	HM Revenue and Customs
HMSO	Her Majesty's Stationery Office

IFLA	International Federation of Library Associations and Institutions
IFPI	International Federation of the Phonographic Industry
IFRRO	International Federation of Reproduction Rights Organizations
ILL	Inter-Library Loan
IP	Intellectual Property
IPO	Intellectual Property Office
IPPR	Institute for Public Policy Research
IPR	Intellectual Property Rights
ISBN	International Standard Book Number
ISP	Internet Service Provider
ISSN	International Standard Serial Number
JISC	Joint Information Systems Committee
LACA	Libraries and Archives Copyright Alliance
MLE	Managed Learning Environment
MP3	MPEG-1/2 audio layer 3 (MPEG stands for Moving Picture Experts Group; MP3 is an audio compression algorithm)
NCA	National Council on Archives
NLA	Newspaper Licensing Agency
OCR	Optical Character Recognition
OECD	Organization for Economic Co-operation and Development
OPSI	Office of Public Sector Information
PDF	Portable Document Format
PLS	Publishers' Licensing Society
PSI	Public Sector Information
PSIH	Public Sector Information Holder
RMI	Rights Management Information
RRO	Reproduction Rights Organization
SHERPA	Securing a Hybrid Environment for Research Preservation and Access
TASI	Technical Advisory Service for Images
TPM	Technical Protection Measures
TRIPS	Trade Related Aspects of Intellectual Property Rights

UCC	Universal Copyright Convention
UNESCO	United Nations Educational, Scientific and Cultural Organization
VLE	Virtual Learning Environment
WATCH	Writers, Artists, and Their Copyright Holders
WCT	WIPO Copyright Treaty
WIPO	World Intellectual Property Organization
WTO	World Trade Organization
XML	Extensible Markup Language

Legal cases

Glossary

Abandonware The situation where copyright ownership gets lost when, for example, businesses go bankrupt or merge

Communication to the public This is an act restricted by copyright in a work; it refers to broadcasting the work or making available to the public the work by electronic transmission in such a way that members of the public may access it from a place and at a time individually chosen by them

Copyright acquis The body of European Union law on copyright and related rights

Database A collection of independent works, data or other materials that are arranged in a systematic or methodical way and are individually accessible by electronic or other means (Directive 96/9/EC)

Database right A property right ('database right') subsists in a database if there has been a substantial investment in obtaining, verifying or presenting the contents of the database (Copyright and Rights in Databases Regulations 1997: SI 1997/3032)

Dealt with An accessible copy made under the exception for visual impairment is an infringing copy if it is dealt with: sold, let for hire, offered or exposed for sale or hire or communicated to the public by electronic means

Deep linking Creating a hyperlink which directs web users to a page within a website without first visiting the home page of that site

Digital rights management system A system which uses digital technologies in order to manage intellectual property rights

Extraction The transfer of the contents of the database to another medium

Legal deposit The legal requirement for publishers to deposit with the British Library and the five copyright libraries (University Library in Cambridge, the Bodleian Library in Oxford, Trinity College Dublin and the national libraries of Scotland and Wales) a single copy of each publication

Lending Making available for use, for a limited period of time and not for direct or indirect economic or commercial advantage (Directive 2006/115/EC codified version, replacing 92/100/EEC)

On demand Interactive on-demand services are characterised by the fact that members of the public may access them from a place and at a time individually chosen by them

Orphan works Works where the rightsholder is difficult or even impossible to identify or locate

Prescribed library The definition of prescribed library as set out in Part A of Schedule 1 to the Copyright (Librarians and Archivists) (Copying of Copyright Material) Regulations 1989: SI 1989/1212 makes it clear that the library must be not for profit. The list set out in the Regulations includes:

- public libraries
- national libraries
- libraries of educational establishments
- parliamentary or government libraries
- local government libraries
- 'Any other library conducted for the purpose of facilitating or encouraging the study of bibliography, education, fine arts, history, languages, law, literature, medicine, music, philosophy, religion, science (including natural and social science) or technology, or administered by any establishment or organization which is conducted wholly or mainly for such a purpose'
- any library outside the UK which exists wholly or mainly to encourage the study of the above subjects

Public domain The public domain comprises the body of all creative works and other knowledge – writing, artwork, music, science, inventions and others – in which no person or organization has any proprietary interest (proprietary interest is typically

represented by a copyright or patent) (source:
http://en.wikipedia.org/wiki/public_domain)

Public sector information Public sector information is any
information that is produced by a public sector body ('public
sector body' is defined in Regulation 3 of the Re-use of Public
Sector Information Regulations 2005)

Rental Making available for use for a limited period of time, for
direct or indirect economic or commercial advantage (Directive
2006/115/EC codified version, replacing 92/100/EEC)

Re-utilization Making available to the public the contents of a
database

Rights management information Information provided by the
copyright owner which identifies the work, the author or any
other rightsholder, or information about the terms and conditions
of use of the work

Safe copying limits When a single copy of an item is made under the
exception of fair dealing for non commercial research or private
study, the safe copying limits are usually taken to be: one chapter
or 5% (whichever is the greater) or one journal article. However,
the fair dealing exception as set out in the CDPA 1988 is not as
specific as this – it certainly doesn't, for example, give a set
percentage that is acceptable in all circumstances

Screenshots Screen captures which could, for example, be of a web
page or a software package

Technical protection measures Any technology, device or
component that, in the normal course of its operation, is designed
to prevent or restrict acts, in respect of works or other subject
matter, which are not authorized by the rightholder of any
copyright

Visually impaired persons Section 6(9) of the Copyright (Visually
Impaired Persons) Act 2002 defines the phrase 'visually impaired
person' as meaning a person:

(a) who is blind;

(b) who has an impairment of visual function which cannot be improved, by the use of corrective lenses, to a level that would normally be acceptable for reading without a special level or kind of light;

(c) who is unable, through physical disability, to hold or manipulate a book; or

(d) who is unable, through physical disability, to focus or move his eyes to the extent that would normally be acceptable for reading.

The definition does not cover dyslexia.

Introduction

In the UK the main piece of legislation governing copyright law is the Copyright Designs and Patents Act 1988 (CDPA 1988), which has been amended many times since receiving royal assent. There isn't, however, an Act of Parliament specifically addressing copyright in a digital era – a 'Digital Copyright Act'. This book aims to consider how copyright law applies to materials in a digital form, and to highlight those instances where content in machine-readable form is treated differently from hard copy content.

Copyright protection is automatic. There is no official registration system for copyright in the UK. There are no forms to be completed, nor are there any fees to be paid in order to get copyright protection. The downside of this is the fact that, as a consequence, there is no central, comprehensive database of rightsholders and how to contact them.

If the UK were to introduce a statutory register of copyright works and their owners this would be in contravention of our obligations under the Berne Convention, which is the main international instrument governing copyright matters (see also pages xxii–xxiii and 112). Nevertheless, Recommendation 14b of the Gowers Report[1] stated that the Patent Office (now known as the UK Intellectual Property Office, or IPO) should establish a voluntary register of copyright either on its own, or through partnerships with database holders, by 2008.

Copyright is an intellectual property right. As with other forms of property, it can be bought and sold. In order to be worthwhile, any register of copyright works and their owners would therefore need to be actively maintained in order to capture the details of any changes in the ownership of the copyright works that it lists, because it is imperative that the ownership data held on such a register is both up to date and accurate.

While it is true that copyright protection is automatic, there are actually several criteria which will determine whether or not a work qualifies for copyright protection:

1 It must be original. It must not have been copied from something that already exists. The requirement of originality has been explored by judges in a number of court cases from which we can deduce that in order to qualify as being original, a work must be the result of the expenditure by the author of skill, judgement and experience, or labour, skill and capital.

2 It must be fixed in a material form. In practice, this means it must be in a form from which it can be reproduced or copied. Copyright doesn't protect ideas as such, it only protects things once they have been 'fixed' in some form.

3 The author must be a qualified person[2] (a British subject or someone who normally lives or is domiciled here, or the material must first be published in this country).

4 The work needs to fall into one of the categories of material protected by copyright:
   • literary works – this includes computer programs (software), e-mails and some databases
   • dramatic works
   • musical works
   • artistic works
   • published editions of literary, dramatic or musical works, because the typographical arrangement will have copyright protection
   • sound recordings
   • films – this includes DVDs and videos
   • broadcasts (although this excludes most websites – see Chapter 2.1).

There is no requirement to put the copyright symbol on the work in order for it to attract copyright protection. This is because one of the principles of the 1886 Berne Convention for the Protection of Literary and Artistic Works is that of automatic protection – national treatment is not dependent on any formality.

Berne Copyright Convention

Article 5 – rights guaranteed

(1) Authors shall enjoy, in respect of works for which they are protected under this Convention, in countries of the Union other than the country of origin, the rights which their respective laws do now or may hereafter grant to their nationals, as well as the rights specially granted by the Convention.

(2) The enjoyment and the exercise of these rights shall not be subject to any formality.

(Source: http://www.wipo.int/treaties/en/ip/berne/trtdocs_wo001.html)

Nevertheless, it is useful to mark your work with the international copyright symbol © followed by your name as the copyright owner and also the year of publication. This will assist you in infringement proceedings, and will be needed in a few foreign countries (albeit that, to the author's knowledge, there are only two countries that are signatories to the Universal Copyright Convention – which does require the © symbol to be used in order to have copyright protection – but not also signatories to the Berne Convention, which doesn't require any formality for works to attract copyright protection: Cambodia and Laos).

It is also worth mentioning that while we do have legislation on 'legal deposit', copyright protection is not dependent upon supplying a copy of the work under the legal deposit procedures.

Copyright featured in the UK's 2005 general election. The Labour Party Manifesto, *Britain Forward Not Back*, stated:

We will modernise copyright and other forms of protection of intellectual property rights so that they are appropriate for the digital age. We will use our presidency of the EU to look at how to ensure content creators can protect their innovations in a digital age. Piracy is a growing threat and we will work with industry to protect against it.

This manifesto commitment led to the Chancellor of the Exchequer commissioning the Gowers Review in the 2005 Pre-Budget Report. Andrew Gowers was asked to establish whether the UK's intellectual property system was fit for purpose in an era of globalization, digitization and increasing economic specialization. The Review was charged with examining all the elements of the IP system – not just copyright – to ensure that it delivers incentives while minimizing inefficiency. Its terms of reference were to consider:

- the way in which government administers the awarding of IP rights and its support to consumers and business
- how well businesses are able to negotiate the complexity and expense of the copyright and patent system, including copyright and patent licensing arrangements, litigation and enforcement
- whether the current technical and legal IP infringement framework reflects the digital environment, and whether provisions for 'fair use' by citizens are reasonable.

Addressing the question of whether the UK's intellectual property system was fit for the digital age, the Gowers Review[1] said that the answer was a qualified 'yes'. Andrew Gowers said:

> I do not think the system is in need of radical overhaul. However, taking a holistic view of the system, I believe there is scope for reform to serve better the interests of consumers and industry alike.

There are three areas in which the Review concentrates its recommendations to improve the UK framework for innovation:

- strengthening the enforcement of IP rights, through clamping down on piracy or trade in counterfeit goods
- reducing the costs of registering and litigating IP rights for businesses large and small
- improving the balance and flexibility of IP rights to allow individuals, businesses and institutions to use content in ways consistent with the digital age.

The copyright balance

Copyright law attempts to balance competing interests. Article 27 of the Universal Declaration of Human Rights states:

(1) Everyone has the right freely to participate in the cultural life of the community, to enjoy the arts and to share in scientific advancement and its benefits.

(2) Everyone has the right to the protection of the moral and material interests resulting from any scientific literary or artistic production of which he is the author.

This balance was carefully crafted over many years, but the digital world has created a new imbalance. Technology now available makes it possible to make a copy of a work in digital form both cheaply and quickly, and the copy that is made is just as good as the original. Without adequate controls in place to ensure that any copies made are paid for, the interests of rightsholders are threatened. As a result, rightsholders have looked to technology to provide possible solutions. These include the use of digital rights management (DRM) systems, which are now protected by legislation.

DRM systems are highly controversial. They can:

- restrict use of copyrighted material in ways already granted by statutory or common law applying to copyright
- enforce additional restrictions at the discretion of the content's publisher
- monitor consumption and user behaviour
- be withdrawn, thus locking up works that have been sold using that DRM system.

Libraries need to retain access to content in perpetuity: they have a remit to preserve our cultural heritage.

These DRM systems can 'lock digital doors' and create a 'digital lock-up'; the problem is that they also lock the doors against exceptions that users may be entitled to, such as 'fair dealing' or the making of an accessible copy for a visually impaired person.

Notes

1 *Gowers Review of Intellectual Property* (2006) HM Treasury, www.hm-treasury.gov.uk/independent_reviews/gowers_review_intellectual_property/gowersreview_index.cfm.

2 A 'qualified' person is defined in Section 154 of the Copyright Designs and Patent Act 1988:

154.–(1) A work qualifies for copyright protection if the author was at the material time a qualifying person, that is –

(a) a British citizen, a British Dependent Territories citizen, a British National (Overseas), a British Overseas citizen, a British subject or a British protected person within the meaning of the British Nationality Act 1981, or

(b) an individual domiciled or resident in the United Kingdom or another country to which the relevant provisions of this Part extend, or

(c) a body incorporated under the law of a part of the United Kingdom or of another country to which the relevant provisions of this Part extend.

1

Issues specific to digital information

1.1 Is digital different?

When considering how copyright law applies to the electronic environment, it is necessary to ask whether digital content is treated any differently from hard copy content – and if so, how. Many times I have heard people say that copyright law applies in the same way to both hard copy and online material: that it is, in effect, 'technology neutral'.

Even if one could argue that copyright law has in the past applied consistently across both hard copy and online content, I am not sure that this will remain true for much longer. And in any case, the Copyright and Related Rights Regulations 2003 (SI 2003/2498) have introduced a number of additional forms of legal protection in the UK which relate only to electronic information. For example:

- the right of communication to the public (see Chapter 8.2.1)
- making it illegal to circumvent a technical measure (see Chapter 3.3)

- protection for electronic rights management information (see Chapter 3.2).

One example of how electronic information is treated differently within the legislation appears in Recital 40 of the Copyright Directive.[1] While Recitals are not part of the core legislation, nevertheless they appear before the Articles in order to provide useful background and they help to explain what the legislators had in mind when they were drafting the directive. Recital 40 says:

> Member states may provide for an exception or limitation for the benefit of certain non-profit-making establishments, such as publicly accessible libraries and equivalent institutions, as well as archives. However, this should be limited to certain special cases covered by the reproduction right. Such an exception or limitation should not cover uses made in the context of on-line delivery of protected works or other subject-matter. This directive should be without prejudice to the member states' option to derogate from the exclusive public lending right in accordance with article 5 of directive 92/100/EEC.[2] Therefore, specific contracts or licences should be promoted which, without creating imbalances, favour such establishments and the disseminative purposes they serve.

Returning to the question of whether digital is different, clearly the physical formats of electronic materials differ from those in hard copy. Instead of printed books, directories, newspapers, magazines and reports, electronic copyright relates to anything in machine readable form, whether that be CD-ROMs, floppy discs, Adobe PDF documents, online databases, digitized images, e-mails, websites, e-journals, news feeds, e-books, online encyclopaedias and online newspapers.

The business models used by vendors of electronic content are different from those for hard copy items. Electronic content may be free or it could be available only on subscription or on a pay-as-you-go basis. A website could be funded or subsidized by paid advertisements, and/or sponsorship. However, one needs to be careful about information that is available free of charge. Simply because it is provided without charge doesn't mean that the rightsholder has given up their copyright in the content. In short, *the internet is not a copyright free zone*. There are a number of points to bear in mind, and they include the following. You must:

- check the website's copyright notice to see whether it permits the copying that you wish to undertake
- acknowledge the source
- take care to ensure that you reproduce the content accurately
- not use the content in a derogatory or misleading manner
- not use the content to promote your organization's products or services, unless you have explicit permission to do so.

These points recognize the need to respect both the economic and the moral rights of the author (see Chapter 8). Even if content has been published on the internet and is readily accessible, this doesn't automatically give you the right to copy either the whole or extensive parts of that content.

It is best to see if there is a copyright notice which sets out what can and what can't be done. If a document has been posted on a website in a format such as MS Word or Adobe PDF, check whether there is a copyright statement within the document itself which makes clear what copying is permitted. (For more information about copyright and websites see Chapter 2.1).

In the electronic world it is possible to monitor the usage of content in a way that is not possible for hard copy items. For example, digital rights management (DRM) technology can monitor how often an item is accessed; as a consequence rightsholders have the potential to charge for each access.

1.1.1 Rightsholder concerns over digital content

Where content is available in a digital format, rightsholders are understandably nervous about the potential for copyright infringement. This nervousness is attributable to a number of factors:

1 Digital materials are often easy to copy. Compare, for example, the time and effort required to stand over a photocopier in order to

make a complete copy of a 350-page book as opposed to making a copy of the PDF version of that same publication.

2 The copies made are of an extremely high quality. A photocopy of a book, even if you guillotine and then bind the copy, is nowhere near as good as the original from which it is copied, whereas a copy of an item in a digital format will be virtually indistinguishable from the original.

3 The material can be distributed to many people within a matter of seconds. For example, if a report is published in a format such as Adobe PDF, Rich Text Format or MS Word, it can easily be sent as an e-mail attachment to multiple recipients.

4 Copying can be achieved at low or marginal cost. Making a photocopy, for example, incurs costs for the paper and the toner, as well as the staff time involved, whereas the making of a digital copy incurs few if any costs.

1.1.2 Rental and lending

Authors and performers have an exclusive right to authorize or prohibit the rental and lending of their works. The European directive on rental and lending rights[2] was implemented in the UK by the Copyright and Related Rights Regulations 1996 SI 1996/2967.[3]

In the directive, 'rental' means making available for use for a limited period of time and for direct or indirect economic or commercial advantage; 'lending' means making available for use for a limited period of time and not for direct or indirect economic or commercial advantage.

However, the use of terminology such as 'lending' or 'inter-library loan' in the context of electronic content is very misleading. The inter-library loan (ILL) of printed material has long been an accepted activity in the print world, but what does this mean in the electronic world? The term 'loan' suggests that the material will be returned at some point in time, but this only applies to books in the print environment, and not to material in the electronic environment, where a copy of the file is made. Nevertheless, a number of licences for electronic products do contain clauses covering inter-library loans. Below is an example from the terms and conditions for OECD's electronic product 'SourceOECD'. It is worth noting that they make absolutely clear that this clause is only applicable to academic and not-for-profit organizations:

> For Academic and Not-For-Profit Organisations only, Inter-Library Loan, performed electronically, may also be made solely on a noncommercial one-off basis.
> (Source: OECD terms and conditions, 24 March 2004, www.sourceoecd.org)

Electronic products are usually governed by a set of terms and conditions or a licence agreement (see Chapter 6). One of the main obstacles to reaching agreement has been the lack of clear definitions describing how librarians wish to share their resources. It is extremely important to think through precisely what it is that you want the licence to cover, and to articulate that as clearly as possible to the vendor. Librarians and publishers need to be able to understand one another's positions and to try to find workable solutions by defining how they want to use the product as precisely as possible. This will assist both librarians and publishers in negotiations for licences of electronic resources.

Tip
If a library negotiates a licence agreement for a product, and wishes to be able to make it available for inter-library loan, this should be built into the wording of the licence.

1.1.3 How rightsholders protect their interests

It is much easier to infringe copyright when material is available in electronic form, and the consequences of infringement are potentially much more damaging. Rightsholders have, therefore, been understandably nervous about their content being available in electronic form. Consequently, they have adopted a number of strategies to protect their information. These have been pursued at one and the same time.

Strengthen copyright law

Since 1991, eight EU copyright directives have been passed. UK copyright law is largely – although not entirely – driven by developments at a European level. An example of existing copyright laws being strengthened is the extension of the term of copyright protection in the 1990s from the life of the author plus 50 years to life plus 70.

Introduce new protections

Another tactic has been to try and introduce new special forms of protection. An example is the database directive (96/9/EC), which was implemented in the UK through the Copyright and Rights in Databases Regulations (SI 1997/3032) and introduced the *sui generis*[4] protection for databases. The definition of a database given in the regulations is 'a collection of independent works, data or other materials that are arranged in a systematic or methodical way and are individually accessible by electronic or other means' and as such the definition covers both electronic and some hard copy content. In order for a database to qualify for copyright protection, the arrangement of the contents of the database must be original. The test is that they must constitute the author's own intellectual creation by reason of the selection or arrangement of the contents of the database. Meanwhile, in order for a database to qualify for database right, substantial investment must have taken place to obtain, verify and present the contents of the database. Some databases will qualify for both copyright protection and database right protection. However, even if a database does not qualify for copyright protection because its contents do not have sufficient originality, the database might still potentially qualify for database right protection.

Use technology to control access

Yet another tactic has been to use technology, such as DRM systems, in order to control access to copyright materials. Rightsholders may well feel that there are practical problems policing the world wide web. Pursuing and catching those who have disobeyed copyright laws can be both onerous and time-consuming, and many copyright owners look upon technological solutions as a much better alternative to litigation because they can prevent unlawful use of their online content.

Use contract law to govern use of content

Rightsholders also use the law of contract in order to protect their interests. Information in electronic formats is often accompanied by a licence or a set of terms and conditions; this means, in effect, that use of the products is governed by the law of contract rather than by the law of copyright (see Chapter 6). This is significant because contract law is able with very few exceptions to override copyright law.

It has taken years to develop the body of legislation within the field of copyright, but all these attempts to craft a careful balance between various competing interests are usurped at a stroke by rightsholders who require users to sign a licence agreement before they are able to make use of their products.

Make it easier to enforce intellectual property rights

It doesn't matter how many legal protections there are in place if copyright law is one of the most frequently broken laws on the planet, and taking a case to court can be extremely costly. Rightsholders have therefore argued successfully that effective enforcement of intellectual property rights is an important part of innovation and wealth creation, and indeed this has been the subject of the most recent two copyright directives passed by the European Commission.[5] According to the Gowers Review, in the ideal intellectual property system the enforcement of IP should be swift, affordable and judicious.

1.2 Digital signatures

Librarians working in 'prescribed libraries' are entitled to copy on behalf of their users, as long as they comply with the conditions set out in the Copyright (Librarians and Archivists) (Copying of Copyright Material) Regulations 1989: SI 1989/1212. The key thing about these regulations is that a user can ask a prescribed library to make a copy of an article or a reasonable proportion of a published work as long as the user signs a declaration form.

> ## Definition of a prescribed library
>
> The definition of a prescribed library only covers libraries which are not conducted for profit. It includes:
>
> - public libraries
> - national libraries
> - libraries of educational establishments
> - parliamentary or government libraries
> - local government libraries
> - 'Any other library conducted for the purpose of facilitating or encouraging the study of bibliography, education, fine arts, history, languages, law, literature, medicine, music, philosophy, religion, science (including natural and social science) or technology, or administered by any establishment or organisation which is conducted wholly or mainly for such a purpose'
> - any library outside the UK which exists wholly or mainly to encourage the study of the above subjects.
>
> (As set out in Part A of Schedule 1 to the Copyright (Librarians and Archivists) (Copying of Copyright Material) Regulations 1989: SI 1989/1212.)

Prescribed libraries must use a form of wording on the declaration form which is substantially in accordance with that set out in Schedule 2 of the Library Regulations. (It should also be pointed out that the 1989 Regulations were amended by the Copyright and Related Rights Regulations 2003: SI 2003/2498.) On the form, the library user declares that:

a) I have not previously been supplied with a copy of the same material by you or any other librarian;

b) I will not use the copy except for research for a non-commercial purpose or private study and will not supply a copy of it to any other person; and

c) to the best of my knowledge, no other person with whom I work or study has made or intends to make, at or about the same time as this request, a request for substantially the same material for substantially the same purpose.

A librarian who copies material on behalf of a user under the Library Regulations does have protection if it transpires that when completing the declaration form the user made a false statement, and the copy turns out to be an infringing copy. This indemnity relies on Section 37(2) of the CDPA 1988, as enacted by Regulation 4(3) of the Library Regulations. Regulation 4(3) of SI 1989/1212 states: 'Unless the librarian is aware that the signed declaration delivered to him . . . is false in a material particular, he may rely on it as to the matter he is required to be satisfied on . . . before making or supplying the copy.'

If a librarian is asked by a user whether a particular act of copying would be considered commercial rather than non-commercial, the librarian would be best advised to refer the user to the CILIP posters, and to the guidance from the British Library[6] and the Copyright Licensing Agency,[7] rather than get involved in making such a decision for the user. If the librarian were to say that the act of copying was permitted, and it subsequently turned out that this advice was incorrect, they could be held jointly liable for the copyright infringement.

The regulations make it clear that the signature 'must be the personal signature of the person making the request. A stamped or typewritten signature, or the signature of an agent, is NOT acceptable.' So the question arises: would a digital signature be acceptable?

A number of UK organizations have information about electronic signatures on their websites which is either misleading or incorrect. For example, some people make statements such as 'Electronic signatures are not yet valid' or 'Electronic signatures are not acceptable as these are not legal in the UK.' While this isn't the case, the situation isn't easy to explain.

Electronic signatures are legally admissible within the UK, following the enactment of the Electronic Communications Act 2000. The Library Regulations (SI 1989/1212) would accommodate electronic signatures, because the signature of the person must be in writing,[8] and this is defined in Section 178 of the CDPA 1988 as including any form of notation or code, whether by hand or otherwise, regardless of the method by which, or medium in or on which, it is recorded.

Unfortunately, that isn't the whole story. The Library Regulations also require the signature to be personal. It must:

- clearly identify the individual
- not easily be used by others
- be created using means that the signatory can maintain under his or her sole control
- be linked to the data to which it relates in such a manner that any subsequent change of data is detectable
- have a high level of encryption.

The UK Intellectual Property Office takes the view that deciding what form of e-signature would fulfil the criteria is a matter for experts in this area.

Further information

Electronic signatures on copyright declaration forms:

www.cilip.org.uk/professionalguidance/copyright/advice/e-signatures.htm.

➡ Relevant legislation

- the Copyright (Librarians and Archivists) (Copying of Copyright Material) Regulations 1989: SI 1989/1212
- Section 7 of the Electronic Communications Act 2000, which covers electronic signatures and related certificates
- the Electronic Signatures Regulations 2002 (SI 2002/318), which requires that electronic signatures should conform to an 'advanced electronic signature'
- Directive 1999/93/EC of the European Parliament and of the Council of 13 December 1999 on a Community framework for electronic signatures.

1.3 Temporary copies

One useful change brought about by the implementation of the Copyright Directive (2001/29/EC) through the Copyright and Related Rights Regulations 2003 (SI 2003/2498) is that *copies made during normal electronic processes, such as transitory copies made by internet service providers, no longer cause problems.*

Article 5 of the Copyright Directive (2001/29/EC) deals with exceptions and limitations. The directive contains a list of exceptions from which member states can make their selection. The list is exhaustive – that is, members states can only opt to implement exceptions that are on the list; they are not able to add anything else to the list.

However, as well as this list of optional exceptions, there is also one compulsory exception in the directive, which all member states were required to implement. It relates to the making of temporary copies. This compulsory exception was implemented in the UK through the insertion of Section 28A in the CDPA 1988:

> Copyright in a literary work, other than a computer program or a database, or in a dramatic, musical or artistic work, the typographical arrangement of a published edition, a sound recording or a film, is not infringed by the making of a temporary copy which is transient or incidental, which is an integral and essential part of a technological process and the sole purpose of which is to enable
>
> (a) a transmission of the work in a network between third parties by an intermediary; or
> (b) a lawful use of the work; and which has no independent economic significance.

This is designed to cover activities such as web browsing where, by its very nature, the technology makes several copies (the copy on screen as well as the copy in the computer cache).

Prior to this change in the law, strictly speaking it was illegal to browse the internet because of the way in which this generates multiple copies – a copy is created in the computer cache as well as on the computer screen. This is an example of how copyright laws, which have developed over many years, don't fit neatly with the way in which the technologies that are used in everyday life result in the making of copies of copyright-protected content. This change to the law is really a matter of common sense, because in effect it says that the making of these temporary copies is no longer a problem. There are, however, several conditions which must be present in order for the copy to be legal. The copy must be:

- transient or incidental
- an integral and essential part of a technological process the sole purpose of which is transmission in a network between third parties or a lawful use of the work, and has no independent economic significance.

As well as making it legitimate to view websites, this may also make the sending of a faxed copy of a copyright work legal, provided that the intermediate steps have no economic significance. However, sending a fax which is capable of being stored electronically for further use by the person receiving it would not fall into this category.

Notes

1 Directive 2001/29/EC of the European Parliament and the Council of 22 May 2001 on the harmonisation of certain aspects of copyright and related rights in the information society (also know as the 'Info Soc directive', and appears in the *Official Journal* L167/10, 22 June 2001.

2 This directive [92/100/EEC] was replaced by Directive 2006/115/EC.

3 See www.legislation.hmso.gov.uk/si/si1996/uksi_19962967_en_1.htm.

4 'Of its own kind', with unique charateristics. Database right is a *'sui generis'* right, because it is a right that is directed at a unique category of materials – in this case databases.

5 2004/48/EC on the enforcement of intellectual property rights and 2007/?/EC on criminal measures aimed at ensuring the enforcement of intellectual property rights. [At the time of writing – July 2007 – the directive still hadn't been passed, but was expected imminently. The initial document was published as COM (2005)276.]

6 See www.bl.uk/services/information/copyrightfaq.html.

7 See www.cla.co.uk/licensing/bl-cla-faq.doc.

8 Regulation 4(2)(a) of the Library Regulations says: 'no copy of any article or any part of a work shall be supplied to the person requiring the same unless . . . he has delivered to the librarian a declaration in writing, in

relation to that article or part of a work, substantially in accordance with Form A in Schedule 2 to these Regulations and signed in the manner therein indicated'.

2

Categories of digital information

2.1 Websites

Section 1 of the CDPA 1988 sets out various descriptions of 'work' in which copyright subsists. We use the word 'subsists' rather than 'exists' because copyright can only exist in relation to the work that it protects. It cannot exist in and of itself.

The types of work that are protected include:

* literary works
* databases
* dramatic works
* musical works
* artistic works
* sound recordings
* films
* broadcasts.

Copyright also subsists in the typographical arrangement of published editions.

The CDPA 1988 does not, however, treat websites as a special category or species in its own right. Broadcasts are treated as a species within UK copyright law, but the definition of 'broadcast' which appears in the CDPA 1988 (Section 6) specifically excludes nearly all websites, with the exception of 'simulcasts':

(1) . . . an electronic transmission of visual images, sounds or other information which

a. is transmitted for simultaneous reception by members of the public and is capable of being lawfully received by them, or

b. is transmitted at a time determined solely by the person making the transmission for presentation to members of the public

(1A) Excepted from the definition of 'broadcast' is any internet transmission unless it is –

a. a transmission taking place simultaneously on the internet and by other means

b. a concurrent transmission of a live event, or

c. a transmission of recorded moving images or sounds forming part of a programme service offered by the person responsible for making the
transmission, being a service in which programmes are transmitted at
scheduled times determined by that person.

Although websites are not protected as a 'species' in their own right, they
are nevertheless protected in a number of ways. The individual components of a web page or a website are protected. If, for example, a web page
consists of a string of text which is wrapped around a chart, and a short
piece of music plays when the web page loads, then the string of text would
be protected as a literary work, the chart would be protected as an artistic work, the piece of music would be protected as a musical work and the
metadata would be protected as a literary work. Websites are also protected by the right of communication to the public, as set out in Section 20
of the CDPA 1988 (see Chapter 8.1.1 for more information).

Materials that are published on the internet are covered by copyright
protection. The mere fact that there is a vast amount of readily available
information on the web does not somehow mean that it is outside the remit
of copyright protection. So, for example, e-mail messages, material on an
FTP site, a compilation of URLs, a Yahoo!-style subject listing, world wide
web pages and FAQs would each be protected as literary works.

The Legal Deposit Libraries Act 2003 anticipates that in future both
electronic and hard copy content will be preserved by the legal deposit
libraries; there are provisions in the Act which specifically relate to websites.

The Act inserts Section 44A into the CDPA 1988:

(1) Copyright is not infringed by the copying of a work from the internet
by a deposit library or person acting on its behalf if –
  (a) the work is of a description prescribed by Regulations under section
      10(5) of the 2003 Act,
  (b) its publication on the internet, or a person publishing it there, is con-
      nected with the United Kingdom in a manner so prescribed, and
  (c) the copying is done in accordance with any conditions so prescribed.

However, as yet no such regulations have been issued.

➡ Relevant legal cases
Agence France-Presse v Google

Background: In March 2005 Agence France-Presse filed a lawsuit against Google alleging that 'Google News' redistributed its story excerpts and photographs without permission, and that it therefore infringed AFP's copyright.

The issues raised by this case have profound implications for the internet, especially because with the rise in popularity of weblogs anyone can be a publisher.

A number of search engines have free news services which aggregate content from thousands of sources; there is always the potential that other rightsowners will take legal action against the search engines. (Other examples include a group of Belgian newspaper publishers, Copiepresse, which took out a similar action in the Belgian courts; and a separate dispute between The Associated Press and Google which resulted in the two companies announcing a new business relationship under which Google will pay AP for news and photos, but the financial details of this arrangement were not disclosed.)

Once the lawsuit was filed, Google removed AFP content from the Google News website. However, this did not deter AFP from pursuing legal action on the grounds that damage had already been done to its business. AFP also said that despite repeated requests for Google to take AFP content off the site, these had all been ignored and Google only took the content down when the lawsuit was filed.

The outcome of the lawsuit hinged on whether AFP could prove that its business had been damaged by Google's redistribution of the content. AFP generates sales by charging media clients subscription fees to republish the content produced by its reporters and photographers. Google argued that the redistribution of AFP news on its sites had actually benefited AFP by providing global exposure.

Outcome: In April 2007 it was announced that Google and Agence France-Presse had signed a licensing deal and settled their lawsuit. Under the agreement, Agence France-Presse will allow Google to post news and photos from AFP journalists. The financial details of the settlement were not disclosed. The deal permits Google to use headlines and photos on Google News and other services that drive online traffic to sites displaying AFP news. The companies did not disclose where else AFP's news would be used by Google.

2.1.1 Copying website designs

The website www.pirated-sites.com provides numerous examples of internet sites that have been copied without permission. This begs the question: how can website owners protect themselves?

There is a website called Copyscape (www.copyscape.com) which is dedicated to defending people's rights online, helping them fight online plagiarism and content theft. The Copyscape service finds sites that have copied content without permission, as well as those that have quoted you.

There are other measures you might want to consider to protect your rights. For example, some people include information within their website's metadata which is not actually required for the website to work, but if someone copied the site this redundant information buried within the metadata would provide useful evidence to show that the site had indeed been copied.

Further information

Pollitt, Michael (2005) Web Design is a Real Steal, *The Independent*,
    (9 March), http://news.independent.co.uk/sci-tech/article5289.ece.

2.1.2 Deep linking

There are two types of link:

- a shallow link provides a link to a home page
- a deep link directs web users to a page within a website without going first to the home page of that site.

There is no express law in the UK forbidding either deep or shallow linking to a third party's website unless permission has been granted. To

Things to consider when deep linking

- Don't skip banner ads.
- Don't circumvent terms and conditions of use.
- Avoid using frames technology – you could be accused of 'passing off' other people's material as though it were your own.
- Avoid using another company's logo as the link.
- Deep linking can be an infringement of database right.

describe permission as being in any way a legal requirement for deep linking goes much further than either current legislation or case law suggests.

To turn almost every web link into an act of copyright infringement would threaten the unique value of the web as a tool of knowledge by preventing people from finding their way around it. If deep linking were illegal, how could search engines exist? Nevertheless, it is advisable to take care over the use of deep links. There are several things worth mentioning:

- **Banner ads.** Since the home page of a website is usually the most frequently visited page for that site, it is where the site is most likely to display banner advertisements. A site might be paid on the basis of the number of 'click-throughs' – that is, the number of times that an advertisement is clicked on. It could be argued that anyone who creates a deep link to a page within a website which has banner ads on its home page is depriving the website of potential income, because anyone who follows the deep links isn't being given the opportunity to see the advertisements.
- **Terms and conditions of use.** On some websites there is a set of terms and conditions of use which specifically states that the site owner does not permit deep links. By deep linking to a page within such a site, you are not giving the user a chance to see that the terms and conditions tell people not to deep link. There are arguments to be considered regarding whether a set of terms and conditions of this kind can be considered as an enforceable contract. However, whether or not this would constitute an enforceable contract, it would certainly not be in the spirit of good netiquette.

- **Frames technology**. Some web pages make use of frames technology, and what looks like a single page is actually made up of several component parts. In such a scenario, it would be possible for at least one of those elements to be from an external site. Without proper labelling, it wouldn't be clear to the user that this was the case (unless they used the mouse to right-click then selected 'Properties' in order to see the URL of that element). As such this could constitute trying to 'pass off' someone else's content as though it were your own.
- **Company logos as links**. Making a copy of a company logo and using it as the place to click on a web page in order to reach a deep link, without the explicit consent of the company, would infringe a company's trademark.

People should be very cautious about deep linking. The best advice, therefore, is to avoid deep linking to other sites without first obtaining the permission of the owners of those sites (see Figure 2.1). If this advice is not heeded, then you could end up having to pay compensation and also making amendments to your website.

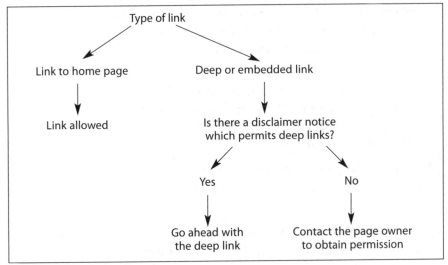

Figure 2.1 Web links – flow chart

Deep linking: best practice guidelines

- Link to the home page if that is sufficient.
- If you want to deep link, first seek permission.
- Check out the website to see if there is a document (usually headed something like 'Disclaimer', 'Liability', 'Copyright' or 'Terms and conditions') which sets out the website's policy regarding the use of deep links.
- Avoid the use of frames technology.
- Use text links.
- Do not use an image of the company logo as the link without first getting permission.

Obtaining permission to deep link

XYZ university provides its students with links to useful websites. Normally we link to the home page of other websites using a text link, providing full acknowledgement and opening the link up in a separate browser window. Sometimes, however, it is more useful for our students if we are able to make a deep link. We are therefore writing to you in order to request permission to make a deep link to the URL listed below:
http://www.abc.com/directory/subdirectory/document.html

In order to avoid the need to contact you for each individual link, please indicate below if you are willing to give us blanket permission to make further deep links to pages on your website if we wish to add further links from our site.

a) Yes, but only if the links are added to an intranet or other networked resource which cannot be accessed externally ❑
b) Yes, regardless of whether the links are placed on an internally or externally accessible site ❑

Many thanks for your assistance.

If you maintain a website, you may wish to develop a policy statement on deep linking. It would be worth looking at how others have dealt with this issue. The HM Revenue & Customs website is a useful example; it has a linking policy which covers both the issue of people wanting to set up deep

Links policy example: HM Revenue & Customs

Links to external websites: HMRC is not responsible for the contents or reliability of any other websites to which we provide a link and does not necessarily endorse the views expressed with them. Listing should not be taken as endorsement of any kind. We cannot guarantee that these links will work at all times and have no control over the availability of the linked pages. In particular HMRC is not responsible for any privacy policies on external websites and we recommend you read the relevant statements on any other websites your visit. HMRC is not responsible for the direct or indirect consequences of you linking to any other website from this website.

You do not have to ask permission to link directly to pages hosted on this site. We do not object to you linking directly to the information that is hosted on our site. However, we do not permit our pages to be loaded into frames on your site. HMRC pages must load into the user's entire window. In order to help you link to our site we have created a button that you may use for this purpose. (See http://www.hmrc.gov.uk/linking/index.htm)

links to the HMRC website and the question of links from the HMRC website to external sites.

There are a number of deep linking agreements available on the web. A quick search of the web brings up examples such as:

- guide to connecting to other websites (includes a deep linking agreement), http://fairuse.stanford.edu/Copyright_and_Fair_Use_Overview/chapter6/6-c.html
- Project Management Institute – linking agreement, www.pmi.org/info/linkagreement.asp
- Autozone.com linking agreement, www.autozone.com/images/terms_conditions/linking_agr071100.pdf
- California Avocado Commission license agreement, www.avocado.org/links/cac_license_agreement.pdf
- the National Association of Realtors' terms and conditions, http://digbig.com/4sqsy.

There are also examples of what not to do – some of which are shown on the site 'Don't Link to Us: stupid linking policies' (www.dontlinktous.com).

➡ Relevant legal cases

Shetland Times Ltd v Dr Jonathan Wills and Zetnews [1996] (Edin Ct Sess) SCLR 160

The weekly *Shetland Times* newspaper sought a permanent ban on certain kinds of unsolicited hypertext links from the *Shetland News*, a daily internet news magazine. The *Shetland News* reproduced verbatim a number of headlines appearing the *Shetland Times*. These headlines were hyperlinked. Clicking on the headline took the reader directly to the internal page on the *Shetland Times* site on which the related story was found. The court stated that:

> access to the pursuer's [*Shetland Times*] items . . . can be obtained by by-passing the pursuers' front page and accordingly missing any advertising material which may appear on it.

The case is a Scottish case, and it does not set a legal precedent because it only reached the interim injunction stage. The case was settled out of court on 11 November 1997, with each side paying its own legal costs. The *Shetland News* agreed that links to stories from the *Shetland Times* would in future only be made under the following conditions:

- Each link to an individual story would be acknowledged by the legend 'A Shetland Times Story' appearing underneath the headline, in the same or similar size type as the headline.
- Adjacent to any such headline(s) would appear a button showing legibly the Shetland Times masthead logo.
- The legend and the button would each be hypertext links to the *Shetland Times* online headline page.

NVM v De Telegraaf (2002)

This Dutch case was brought to the Supreme Court on the grounds of database right infringement. The Dutch newspaper *De Telegraaf* owned a website called El Cheapo. The site had a search engine which could be used to search for bargains on the internet. Included in the searchable information were datafiles from the Dutch Real Estate Agents' Association (NVM). The NVM argued this was an infringement of its database rights.

The claim failed on the grounds that the datafiles did not constitute a database under the relevant Dutch legislation.

Ticketmaster Corp. v Tickets.com[1] (2000)

Tickets.com is an online provider of entertainment, sports and travel tickets. It provided hypertext links to Ticketmaster web pages for tickets that were not available at Tickets.com.

Ticketmaster sued Tickets.com, claiming that such links constituted copyright infringement, among other claims. Indeed, it sued Tickets.com for:

- copyright infringement
- unfair competition
- reverse 'passing off'
- false advertising
- unfair business practices
- misappropriation
- trespass
- unjust enrichment
- breach of contract
- interference with business advantage.

On 27 March 2000, federal judge Harry L. Hupp for the Central District Court of California issued a first ruling in favour of Tickets.com. In his ruling, Hupp concluded that hypertext linking 'does not itself involve a violation of the Copyright Act . . . since no copying is involved'.

Stepstone v OfiR (2001)

The Danish media company OfiR had deep-linked from its website into the website of the online recruitment company Stepstone. A German court granted an injunction to Stepstone preventing OfiR from deep linking into the Stepstone website.

PCM v Kranten.com (2001)

PCM operated a website which contained news items. Kranten.com then set up hyperlinks in the form of headlines which linked straight from their own website to the full news item on PCM's site, bypassing the claimant's home page. PCM argued that Kranten.com was infringing its copyright and database rights. These claims were rejected by the court, which held that PCM had put insufficient effort into composing the collection of headlines for them to constitute a database. The claim of copyright infringement also failed, because under Dutch law news agencies were allowed to copy articles. The Dutch court also suggested that PCM could have constructed its website so that its advertisements were not only viewed from its home page.

SNC Havas Numerique v SA Kelijob (2001)

SNC, an online employment site, brought an action against Kelijob, an employment search engine, alleging copyright infringement and unfair competition. The defendant had provided links to the plaintiff's site without authorization. In this particular deep linking case, the French court granted an injunction and distinguished between surface linking, in which there is an implied right due to the nature of the internet, and deep linking, which requires authorization.

Haymarket v Burmah Castrol (2001)

Publishing firm Haymarket started a legal action against Burmah Castrol for infringement of online intellectual property rights. The dispute related to links from Burmah Castrol's Complete-Motoring.com website to two of Haymarket's websites – whatcar.com and autosport.com. These websites were displayed within a Castrol-branded border when users clicked on a link saying 'Magazines' on Castrol's website.

The problem concerned the use of frames technology, because this could have given the impression that the linked companies were associated with one another when they were not, which might potentially lead to damage to Haymarket's reputation or brand value.

Legal proceedings were threatened against Burmah Castrol by Haymarket Interactive Limited for this unauthorized framing. The company's lawyers wrote to Burmah requesting that the framing stop as it constituted passing off and copyright and trademark infringement, and also that Burmah pay damages for Haymarket's lost content revenue. The case was eventually settled out of court.[2]

Kelly v Arriba Soft Corporation (280 F. 3d 934 (CA9 2002) *withdrawn*, re-filed at 311 F. 3d 811 (CA9 2003))

Ditto (formerly known as Arriba Soft) operated a 'visual search engine' located at www.ditto.com. The search engine searched millions of photographs and displayed its search results in the form of small (or thumbnail) pictures which were obtained by Arriba by copying the images from other websites.

Les Kelly was a photographer of the American West. Among the pictures indexed on the Ditto website were a number of images belonging to Mr Kelly. In addition to thumbnails of images, it was also possible for a ditto.com user to view larger versions of the same picture within the context of Arriba's website, and these larger versions were imported directly from the website of Les Kelly.

Mr Kelly sued Arriba for copyright infringement saying that Arriba had reproduced miniatures of his images without his permission, and that it used these to link to his original photographs.

A three-judge panel of the appeals court held that use of the thumbnail pictures fell within the fair use defence because they were small, low resolution images that were used for a different purpose than Kelly's works, which were artistic images used for illustrative purposes.

However, in a much more far-reaching ruling, the court decided that Ditto could not send users to the original photo through a link. It was the first time an appellate court had ruled on the issue of 'in-line linking' or 'framing' (the practice followed by many search engines of providing a link that opens a browser window displaying material from another website). The court held that Arriba's online linking and framing of Kelly's full-sized images had infringed Mr Kelly's exclusive right to display the copyrighted works publicly.

Danish Newspaper Publishers Association v Newsbooster (Denmark 7/5/2002, Copenhagen Bailiff's Court)

Newsbooster was a news-oriented website which provided links to news articles in more than 3,000 sites. It was akin to a news channel on a search engine, except that it charged a subscription fee and let users choose to receive links automatically by e-mail.

The Danish Newspaper Publishers Association took action against Newsbooster for copyright infringement, claiming that Newsbooster violated copyright law by deep linking to newspaper articles on a number of Danish websites. The Danish court ruled in favour of the Danish Newspaper Publishers Association, saying that a website cannot provide hyperlinks to certain pages of another site without the site owner's permission.

British Broadcasting Corporation v Hendrik Noorderhaven (2005)

The BBC sent a cease and desist order to a Dutch website which enables users to search content from the BBC's teletext service.

The BBC only offers a limited version of its Ceefax service on the continent. Hendrik Noorderhaven got a friend based in the UK to capture the data using a PCTV card. Mr Noorderhaven created a website (www.ceefax.tv) which receives and uploads data published in the UK and continental users are then able to search the data.

The ceefax.tv website attracts over 15,000 daily web visitors, and Mr Noorderhaven says that he is doing no more than Google does by capturing the data, indexing it and enabling users to query it. The site does make clear that Ceefax is a trademark of the BBC. However, the BBC demanded closure of the website, claiming copyright infringement.[3]

Further information

DTI Consultation Document on the Electronic Commerce Directive: the liability of hyperlinkers, location tool services and content aggregators, June 2005, www.dti.gov.uk/files/file13986.pdf, and the government response at www.dti.gov.uk/files/file35905.pdf, December 2005.

2.1.3 Podcasts

A podcast is a digital media file, or a series of such files, that is distributed over the internet using syndication feeds for playback on portable media players and personal computers.

(Source: http://en.wikipedia.org/wiki/Podcasting)

Podcasts don't seem to fall within the definition of a broadcast. It seems likely that they would be protected under copyright law, not as a specific entity/species but rather in their component parts – for example, the soundtrack as a sound recording. They would also be protected by the right of communication to the public.

WIPO were due to pass a Broadcasting Treaty during the course of 2007, and early discussions did consider extending the treaty to cover activities such as webcasting or podcasting. However, a number of podcasting organizations lobbied against such a change. At the time of writing it looks as though plans for a new Treaty have been shelved for the moment.

Further information

Sutter, Gavin (2007) Podcasts and the Law, *JISC Legal*, (11 April), www.jisclegal.ac.uk/publications/podcasts.htm.

2.1.4 E-mail correspondence

In Cembrit Blunn Ltd & Anor v Apex Roofing Services LLP & Anor [2007] EWHC 111 (Ch), the judge made clear that business letters can be protected by copyright and that to forward them to other people can be an infringement.

Not every letter or e-mail will have copyright protection, because this is reserved for works which involve original skill or labour and which do not involve copying the work of another person. Originality in this context does not require the work to be an original or inventive thought; rather, it requires originality in the expression of that thought. Where existing subject matter is used by an author, independent skill must be applied to justify copyright protection for a resulting work.

In the case of Cembrit Blunn Ltd & Anor v Apex Roofing Services LLP, Dansk Eternit Holdings wrote a letter to Cembrit Blunn. A copy of the letter was subsequently provided to Apex Roofing by a third party who had been given it by Cembrit in the course of a professional relationship that they had with Cembrit.

Cembrit Blunn and Dansk brought an action for breach of copyright and misuse of confidential information, claiming that Apex Roofing was not entitled to copy or circulate the letter because it was a copyright work and was confidential to Cembrit and Dansk.

Apex alleged that the third party who had passed a copy of the letter to them was free to circulate copies of the letter. The judge disagreed, as he felt that the letter had clearly been communicated in circumstances that imposed an obligation of confidence. The judge concluded that there was no doubt that it was possible for copyright to subsist in business correspondence generally, although there might be some question about what implied licences were given with regard to the reproduction of the correspondence.

Further information

Forwarding an Email can Infringe Copyright, *Out-law News*, (14 February 2007), www.out-law.com/default.aspx?page=7768.

Snow, Ned (2007) A Copyright Conundrum: protecting email privacy, *Kansas Law Review*, 55, 101, University of Arkansas, http://papers.ssrn.com/sol3/papers.cfm?abstract_id=981729.

2.2 E-books

2.2.1 Finding digital books

A number of specialized databases provide information about or access to many thousands of digitized books and texts, some of which are commercial products. Examples include:

- Digital Book Index, http://digitalbookindex.org
- The Online Books Page, http://digital.library.upenn.edu/books
- Digital Media Locator, http://ebooklocator.com

- eBooks, www.ebooks.com
- NetLibrary, www.netlibrary.com.

2.2.2 Illegal sale of e-books

In a number of cases, enterprising individuals have sold illegal copies of digital content on the internet through auction websites. In one case, for example, the publisher John Wiley & Sons filed lawsuits against a number of individuals who engaged in the unlawful sale of their copyrighted products through the eBay auction website.[4]

The legal action alleged that these individuals had sold pirated electronic copies of books which were available in retail markets as well as pirated copies of manuals which were distributed by Wiley solely to professors free of charge.

By the time Wiley announced its legal action in March 2005, two of the cases had already resulted in default judgments in favour of Wiley to the tune of $18,417 and $24,398.50 respectively.

Meanwhile, dissertations that are openly published on university websites have been sold to students by people who pass these off as their own work. This is a new facet to the increasing problem of plagiarism in higher education. Web-based auction sites have been found to sell dozens of postgraduate dissertations for as little as £10 each. Apart from removing the dissertations from the public domain, university managers feel at a loss as to what measures they can take to counter this scam.

2.2.3 E-books and publishers

According to the Society of Authors (2003), e-book royalties should be much higher than royalties on traditional books. Some publishers ask for permissions to be cleared for 'all forms and editions', even where a more limited licence would be sufficient. Copyright can often be a bundle of rights, and so if one wants to copy a single item, it could require clearance for several rights within that one item. The reference to 'permissions to be cleared' is really all about ensuring that all the required permissions are sought and granted. When an e-book is produced, the publisher is probably going to want to control all of the rights, but the Society of Authors recommends that authors should retain electronic rights other than e-book rights, or at least that the contract should stipulate that these rights will only be exploited with the agreement of the author at that time.

Further information

Department of Trade and Industry and Publishers Association (2002) *Combating Internet Copyright Crime*, www.publishers.org.uk/paweb/paweb.nsf/0/b789b8f162d0e00180256cd800 3b259b/$file/internet%20piracy.pdf.

Gould, Alice (2007) The Blogosphere, the Law and the Printed Word, *The Guardian*, (23 April), http://media.guardian.co.uk/ mediaguardian/story/0,,2063100,00.html (free registration required).

IPR Helpdesk (2006) *Copyright and Internet Guide*, www.ipr-helpdesk.org/guias/guia1/en/guia.pdf.

IPR Helpdesk (2006) *Intellectual Property Aspects of World Wide Web Authoring*, www.ipr-helpdesk.org/controlador.jsp?cuerpo= seccionador&seccion=documentos&modo=listado&cod_nodo_padre=t_ 01.05&niveles_profundidad=3&len=en.

IPR Helpdesk (n.d.) *Creating a Website*, www.ipr-helpdesk.org/ controlador.jsp?cuerpo=seccionador&seccion= documentos&modo=listado&cod_nodo_padre=t_01.05&niveles_profund idad=3&len=en.

Olsen, Stefanie (2003) *Google Cache Raises Copyright Concerns*, (9 July), http://news.com.com/2100-1038_3-1024234.html.

Oppenheim, Charles (2000) Does Copyright Have any Future on the Internet? *Journal of Documentation*, **56** (3), 279–98.

Parliamentary Office of Science and Technology (2002), *Copyright and the Internet*, www.parliament.uk/post/pn185.pdf.

Society of Authors (2003) *Quick Guide 8: publishing contracts*.

World Intellectual Property Organization (2002) *Intellectual Property on the Internet: a survey of issues*, www.wipo.int/copyright/en/ecommerce.

2.3 Databases and database right

In a review of digital copyright, it is important to cover database right. However, it is also necessary to point out that the definition of 'database' which appears in the Copyright and Rights in Databases Regulations 1997 is not limited to electronic products. The Regulations say that a database is: 'a collection of independent works, data or other materials that are arranged in a systematic or methodical way and are individually accessible by electronic or other means'.

So, while databases are protected as a 'species', they aren't necessarily digital. The definition would certainly cover many websites. It would also cover collections of material such as directories and encyclopaedias (which could be either hard copy or electronic publications), statistical databases, online collections of journals and multimedia collections.

The Copyright and Rights in Databases Regulations (SI 1997/3032) implement Directive 96/9/EC, which harmonizes the laws of member states relating to the protection of copyright in databases. It introduced a *sui generis* right whose purpose is to prevent the extraction and re-utilization of all or a substantial part of the contents of a database ('database right').

'Extraction' is the transfer of the contents of the database to another medium. The legal definition of 'extraction' in Article 7(2)(a) is the permanent or temporary transfer of all or a substantial part of the contents of the database to another medium by any means or in any form. It covers not only transfer to a medium of the same type but also to one of another type. This means that merely printing out data falls within the definition of 'extraction'.

'Re-utilization' is the making available to the public of the contents of a database. In Article 7 of the directive the term 're-utilization' means any form of making available to the public all or a substantial part of the contents of a database by the distribution of copies, by renting or by online or other forms of transmission.

It would therefore cover not only the making available to the public of the contents of the database directly from the database, but also the making available to the public of works, data or other materials which are derived indirectly from the database, without having access to the database.

2.3.1 How a database qualifies for copyright or database right

A database could potentially be protected by copyright and or by database right. In order for a database to qualify for database right:

- there must have been substantial investment in obtaining, verifying and presenting the contents of the database
- it must be 'original', and it is original only if 'by reason of the selection or arrangement of the contents of the database the database constitutes the author's own intellectual creation (CDPA 1988, as amended by 1997/3032 Copyright and Rights in Databases Regulations 1997).

If the database attracts copyright protection, then this will last for 70 years from the end of the year of death of the author, if there is one, or the end of year of first publication if there is no personal author. If the database qualifies for database right, then the duration of database right is 15 years from creation or from being made available to the public if this occurs during the 15-year period. Any substantial new investment in a database begins a new 15-year term of protection.

2.3.2 Exceptions to database right

While there are over 50 exceptions to copyright, the number of exceptions to database right is considerably smaller. There is still the exception for 'fair dealing'. Fair dealing in the database right is permitted provided that:

- the person extracting the material is a lawful user of the database
- the purpose is illustration for teaching or research and not for any commercial purpose
- the source is indicated.

There are also a number of public administration exceptions which cover parliamentary and judicial proceedings, royal commissions, statutory inquiries and material which is open to public inspection or on an official register.

➡ Relevant legal cases

British Horseracing Board v William Hill (2004) (C-203/02)

This was the first real test of database right, although the topic had been touched upon in earlier court cases.

The BHB maintained a database which was constantly updated. Indeed, the cost of continuing to obtain, verify and present the contents of the database was approximately £4 million per year, involving about 80 staff and extensive computer software and hardware. The database contained details of over a million horses. It consisted of some 214 tables, altogether containing over 20 million records. An estimated total of 800,000 new records or changes to existing records were made each year.

Initially, the British Horseracing Board won a high court challenge against William Hill over the use of pre-race data. BHB had argued that internet bookmakers who wished to use information such as runners and riders should pay a copyright fee. The court decided that the defendant had infringed database right in listing the horses scheduled to run in forthcoming races. It was accepted that there was nothing intellectual or creative involved in making such lists, but since considerable investment had gone into the creation of the lists, database right was justified.

However, the case then went to the Court of Appeal, and in May 2002 the Court of Appeal referred a number of questions concerning the interpretation of the database directive to the European Court of Justice. The main issues on which clarification was sought were:

- What exactly does database right protect?
- When will extraction and/or re-utilization of a database be prohibited?
- What constitutes a substantial part of a database and what constitutes an insubstantial part of a database?
- What do extraction and re-utilization actually mean?

When the European Court of Justice finally delivered its judgment in November 2004, it ruled that William Hill's use of horseracing data did not after all infringe the BHB's database rights. This came as something of a surprise to people following the case, because the Advocate General's opinion had been quite favourable to database owners. Normally, one would expect the ECJ's decisions to follow the opinion given by the Advocate General, but that did not happen in this instance.

The ECJ said that the BHB did not have database right in its database of horse racing data because it had not made a sufficient investment in obtaining the contents of the database. According to the ECJ, 'obtaining' means 'seeking out existing independent materials' rather than 'the creation of materials'. The phrase 'investment in obtaining the contents' of a database was explained by the ECJ in paragraph 31 of its judgment in the following terms:

> ... the expression investment in ... the obtaining ... of the contents of a database must ... be understood to refer to the resources used to seek out existing independent materials and collect them in the database, and not to the resources used for the creation as such of independent materials. The purpose of the protection by the sui generis right provided for by the directive is to promote the establishment of storage and processing systems for existing information and not the creation of materials capable of being collected subsequently in a database.

The BHB had spent considerable time and effort creating the data but the ECJ found that this was simply part of the process of putting together the pre-race information, including name, place and length of races, and details of the horses, and that it did not represent 'investment in ... obtaining'.

The ECJ also clarified what is meant by 'verification' and took pains to distinguish between checking the accuracy of the component data during its creation and its accuracy once a part of the database:

> The expression investment in...the...verification...of the contents of a database must be understood to refer to the resources used, with a view to ensuring the reliability of the information contained in that database, to monitor the accuracy of the materials collected when the database was created and during its operation. The resources used for verification during the state of creation of data or other materials which are subsequently collected in a database, on the other hand, are resources used in creating a database and cannot therefore be taken into account in order to assess whether there was substantial investment in the terms of Article 7(1).

In the cases ruled upon so far by the ECJ, the issue of substantial investment in the presentation of data in a database has been found to be closely linked to the creation of the data itself, such that there has been no useful exposition of where the database right might be created by such investment.

The first owner of the database right is its maker, subject to certain provisions in Regulation 14. Regulation 14 defines the maker as:

> … the person who takes the initiative in obtaining, verifying or presenting the contents of a database and assumes the risk of investing in that obtaining, verification or presentation shall be regarded as the maker of, and as having made, the database.

Further information

IPR Helpdesk (2007) *Database Protection in the EU*, www.ipr-helpdesk.org.

2.4 Screenshots

A screenshot is a screen capture – that is, an image of everything on a screen – which could, for example, be from a web page or a software package.

It is advisable to obtain permission from site owners to use screenshots.

2.4.1 Screenshots of web pages

A web page may well be made up of several component parts such as a string of text, a photograph and a diagram; each of these elements has protection in its own right. Each part will be protected as a literary or artistic

---

Tip

If it is for a non-commercial use, first see whether the rightsowner will give you the necessary permission free of charge, rather than automatically expecting to have to pay a permission fee.

work. The website owner might or might not own each element in a given screenshot, so this would need to be checked.

In order to establish whether you have permission to use a screenshot, it is important to check the web copyright notice in order to see if it includes guidance on the use of screenshots. If it doesn't give the necessary permission, the next step is to contact the rightsholder and to ask whether they will give you permission to use the screenshot.

2.4.2 Screenshots of software

When seeking to licence screenshots of software, you need to be clear about precisely what the licence actually covers. For example, a screenshot of a piece of software might involve not only graphical images included in the software, but also toolbars, fonts and the general look and feel of the software. These elements will therefore need to be included within the scope of any licence.

Whether it is a screenshot of a web page or of software, getting copyright clearance is not always going to be as straightforward as it might at first appear to be. There may be a number of different rights involved, rather than just one. The screenshot may contain:

- original artwork
- text, which has its own copyright protection
- a trademark
- pictures of Equity members or members of the Musicians' Union, in which case a separate fee may be required for use of those images
- a number of photographs, detailed graphics or any other third party material, and each independent work may have to be licensed separately if the website does not own copyright.

2.4.3 Screenshots and moral rights

It is extremely important to avoid:

- inaccurate or misleading labelling of the screenshot

- any suggestion of endorsement by the site owners
- any alteration of the screenshot
- the use of framing in a way which is likely to cause problems with the site owners.

When trying to license screenshots it is especially important to consider the moral rights of the website owner, since any form of derogatory treatment or false attribution in relation to a screenshot could potentially result in a dispute.

Checklist for obtaining copyright clearance in screenshots

- Set out as clearly as possible what copyright material is to be used.
- Be clear about the uses that you intend to make of the screenshot and communicate these to the rightsowner.
- When in doubt, seek permission.
- Always give appropriate acknowledgements.
- Obtain the relevant permissions in writing.

Further information

Morrison, Alex (2004), Briefing Paper on Copyright in Screenshots, *JISC Legal Information Service*, www.jisclegal.ac.uk/pdfs/screenshotscopyright.rtf.

2.5 Images

A wealth of images is available on the internet, and it is easy to copy those to a computer or to a website. Indeed, the ease with which content on the web can be both accessed and copied leads many people to assume that they are at liberty to copy that material, and to use it in any way they want.

Unfortunately, this viewpoint overlooks the need to respect copyright law; anyone who operates on that basis lays themselves – and their employer – open to the potential consequences of infringing copyright.

In a posting on the FreePint Bar (www.freepint.com/go/b84175), for example, one person commented on how they had used some general small business images for their website, sourced from a variety of places, that they thought were free. This led to them receiving a letter from a large firm of solicitors claiming that they had 'used the identified images without proper licence and payment' and had infringed the solicitors' client's copyright. Along with the letter came an invoice and an annual licence agreement for the use of one small image. The invoice was for over £2,500.

An article in the *Guardian* (Grossman, 2007) has explored the way in which big picture agencies are enforcing their copyright and the expensive implications of the unlicensed use of images.

Photographs and images are protected as artistic works within copyright law, irrespective of artistic merit. The only requirements are that these works should be original, and fixed in some form.

It is important to recognize that copyright is an automatic right. There is no requirement for a photographer to go through a formal registration process before his or her work is protected; nor is there any need for it to be marked with a copyright statement. So, if there is an image or a photograph on a website which you want to copy and use on your own website, and you can't see any kind of copyright statement on the website or a © symbol immediately underneath the photograph, you must never assume that this gives you the right to use that picture on your own website.

DOs and DON'Ts

The internet is not a copyright free zone:
- ■ Do seek copyright permission.
- ■ Do acknowledge the source.
- ■ Don't alter the image.

The author as first owner of copyright in a work has a number of economic rights. These give the author the exclusive right to copy the work, make an adaptation of the work, issue copies to the public, perform, show or play the work in public or communicate the work to the public by electronic transmission.

In addition to these economic rights, an author or creator also has a number of moral rights. These include:

- the right of paternity (the right of the author of a work to be acknowledged as the author or creator)

- the right of the author to object to false attribution
- the right not to have his or her work subjected to 'derogatory treatment'.

Within a digital environment, moral rights are particularly important because of the ease with which content can be altered, changed or manipulated. If digital images are reproduced electronically, it is important to ensure that they are reproduced in their entirety unless permission has been secured from the rightsholder.

One important piece of advice, therefore, is 'don't alter the image', because that could infringe an author's right of integrity. If, for example, you were to crop or to stretch an image, this could breach the photographer's right not to have his or her work subjected to 'derogatory treatment'.

In addition to the above moral rights, there is an additional right which is given to the subjects of photographs and films taken for domestic and private purposes. This restricts their subsequent use beyond the purposes for which they were originally taken, without the subjects' consent. If, for example, Joe Bloggs commissioned a professional photographer to take a picture of him, even though the photographer would retain the copyright in the picture that had been taken, the photographer would not be able to publish it without the permission of Joe Bloggs.

It is true that there are a number of copyright exceptions, or permitted acts, which people might turn to in order to justify a particular instance of copying. But these can only be included in our national legislation if they comply with what is commonly referred to as the 'Berne three-step test'. It means that the exceptions only apply:

- in certain special cases
- if they do not conflict with a normal exploitation of the work
- if they do not unreasonably prejudice the legitimate interests of the rightsowner.

In the case of fair dealing for research or private study, for example, it would not be possible to copy someone else's picture to your website or intranet, because that would be the equivalent of multiple copying and could not be justified under those exceptions.

Neither can the fair dealing exception for reporting current events be used, because it specifically excludes the copying of photographs.

There are limited circumstances in which fair dealing for criticism or review can be used for copying a photograph. The case of Fraser Woodward Limited v British Broadcasting Corporation and Brighter Pictures Limited 2005 EWHC 472 (Ch) explored the use of the exception for criticism or review. It relates to the use of photographs of the Beckhams in the BBC's *Tabloid Tales* programme. When considering whether the use of the photographs had been fair for the purposes of the concept of 'fair dealing' the following points were taken into account: their use on screen was not over-long, and use in the context of criticism and review had not been a contrivance merely to justify a use whose purpose was in substance not that of criticism and review.

Case study

A public library has a number of photographs in its local studies collection which have been donated to the library over a number of years. The library decides that it would like to digitize these pictures and publish them on a publicly accessible website. The library is not able to rely on fair dealing to justify the digitization, and indeed would be hard-pressed to find a copyright exception which would give the necessary permission. The library therefore needs to seek the rights both to reproduce and also to communicate to the public the photographs in question.

In most cases, the copyright holder will need to be approached prior to any use of an image that falls beyond the limited exceptions permitted by copyright law.

Getting the necessary copyright clearance can be extremely time-consuming. It is highly likely that there won't be any information about the author of a photograph on the photograph itself. In the case of books and journals, we have had internationally accepted identifiers for many years in the form of the international standard book number (ISBN) and the international standard serial number (ISSN). But this is not the case with photographs, and it can be a tall order first to identify and then to trace the rightsowner.

The Gowers Review (2006) identified the problems relating to what are known as 'orphan works' – copyrighted works whose owners cannot be identified by someone else who wishes to use the work. Indeed, even if an individual or researcher is able to find some information about the author, this may not be sufficient to identify the current rightsowner. When trying to trace copyright owners for work that you wish to use, it is important to bear in mind that copyright is a property right. It can be bought, sold, given away or bequeathed in a will, so ownership can in theory change hands many times. The author may, therefore, have assigned copyright to a third party.

The Gowers Review (2006) proposed an orphan works provision. This would make it easier for creative artists to re-use orphan copyright protected material, thus unlocking previously unusable material. Indeed, the Gowers Review made three recommendations with respect to orphan works:

- Recommendation 13: propose a provision for orphan works to the European Commission, amending directive 2001/29/EC.
- Recommendation 14a: the Patent Office (now known as the UK Intellectual Property Office) should issue clear guidance on the parameters of a 'reasonable search' for orphan works, in consultation with rightsholders, collecting societies, rightsowners and archives, when an orphan works exception comes into being.
- Recommendation 14b: the Patent Office should establish a voluntary register of copyright, either on its own or through partnerships with database holders, by 2008.

2.5.1 Sources of royalty-free pictures

Free stock image collections:
- FreeFoto.com, www.freefoto.com/
- Free Images.co.uk, www.freeimages.co.uk/
- MorgueFile, www.morguefile.com/
- Imageafter, www.imageafter.com/

Creative Commons images:

- Creative Commons search, http://search.creativecommons.org/
- Flickr advanced search, www.flickr.com/search/advanced/.

Creative Commons enables the owner of the copyright – such as a photographer or an author – to change the terms on which their work is protected from 'all rights reserved' to 'some rights reserved', as there are a range of licences for them to choose from to suit their needs. They might, for example, be willing to let their work be copied so long as this is not for a commercial purpose.

Note: you should always check that the terms and conditions on the sites permit you to use of the image as you intend, because they don't all permit commercial use, for example, and there are a number of different types of Creative Commons licences.

Further information

Gowers Review of Intellectual Property (2006), HM Treasury.

Grossman, Wendy M. (2007) A Picture Paints a Thousand Invoices, *Guardian*, (1 February), www.guardian.co.uk/technology/2007/Feb/01/copyright.newmedia.

Technical Advisory Service for Images (TASI), www.tasi.ac.uk.

2.6 Music downloads

Downloading music files from the internet without the permission of the rightsholder(s) is illegal. Rightsholder bodies such as the International Federation of the Phonographic Industry (IFPI) and the British Phonographic Industry (BPI) have been campaigning prominently in the UK to stamp out the sharing of unlawfully copied music. Indeed, they have taken court action to force internet service providers to disclose the details of people alleged to have used peer-to-peer file-sharing services to copy or to share unlawfully copied files.[5]

Internet service providers (ISPs) often refuse to provide details of their users on the grounds that they are bound by their obligations under the Data Protection Act 1998 in relation to personal data about the file sharer. However, disclosure under the Data Protection Act 1998 is possible where a disclosure order is obtained. This kind of order is called a Norwich Pharmacal order because that is the name of the first case where an order of this sort was obtained. When an innocent party gets mixed up in wrong-doing, but has documents or information which is relevant to that wrong-doing, they may be subject to a court order to disclose that information. Usually the party who went to court in order to obtain that information will be required to pay either all or a proportion of the costs (including the legal fees) of the innocent party relating to the application.

It is important for computer users to bear in mind that organizations may well monitor what individuals are doing on their network. This is understandable when one bears in mind that if a network – such as that belonging to a university or a company – discovers that illegal copies of music files are being swapped over or stored on their networks, then the university or the business could find itself liable for infringement.

Tip

Companies would do well to check the wording of their Acceptable Use Policy to ensure that it sets out clearly that the sharing or storage of music, film or other unlawful files is not permitted. They should check their computer networks and local drives in order to establish that no unlawfully copied files are being stored on the network, and they should also periodically remind employees of the Acceptable Use Policy.

Depending on the wording of the policy, downloading unlicensed software, films or music files for non-business purposes could be regarded as computer misuse, and render the employee liable for disciplinary action up to and including dismissal.

One user of a peer-to-peer file-sharing service asked me about music downloading, and whether her use of a particular service was legal. She mentioned that service users could make a voluntary payment, she thought that paying for it would make the download legal. The *BPI Filesharing Factsheet* lists a number of well known file-sharing clients which are used to file share illegally, and – interestingly – the service the enquirer mentioned was one of those listed on the factsheet.

Simply because a service collects money from its users, this doesn't automatically mean that some or all of this money is being forwarded to the rightsholder. And if the payment is made on a voluntary basis, how can the rightsholder be guaranteed a payment for each use of their work? Questions to consider include:

- Does any of the money go to the rightsholder?
- If the rightsholder requires payment for each digital copy made of their work, how can this be guaranteed if the money is collected on a voluntary basis?
- Has the file-sharing client got an agreement with the appropriate rightsholders to act on their behalf?

➡ Relevant legal cases

Sony Music Entertainment (UK) Limited and others v EasyInternetcafé Limited (High Court, 28 January 2003) [2003] EWHC 62 (Ch)

EasyInternetcafé was found guilty of copyright infringement for allowing customers to download music from the internet onto CDs.

Customers using a terminal in one of the internet cafés could download files from the internet and store them on the central server in a private directory. The private directory was cross referenced with a user ID that the customer had been given. Members of staff at the internet café were not permitted to look at the contents of the files which had been saved to the central server without the customer's permission. The customer then paid a fee of £5. This charge was made up of £2.50 for the CD and £2.50 for the copying service.

EasyInternetcafé said that it provided a significant number of warnings to customers about copyright infringement. However, sections 16 and 17 of the CDPA 1988 make it clear that even if you do not know that what you are doing is unlicensed, you will still infringe copyright. Section 16(2) specifically says:

Copyright in a work is infringed by a person who without the licence of the copyright owner does, or authorises another to do, any of the acts restricted by the copyright.

Even though staff at EasyInternetcafé were not permitted to look at the contents of the customer's private directory without that customer's permission, the record companies had evidence of at least one occasion when staff did see precisely what was being downloaded.

EasyInternetcafé tried to defend their action using Section 70 (the time-shifting principle) of the CDPA 1988, which permits consumers for private and domestic purposes to make recordings of television programmes with their video recorders in order to watch them at a more convenient time, arguing that this was what consumers were doing with music downloaded in their internet cafés. Mr Justice Peter Smith rejected the argument on the grounds that staff at the internet café were downloading the music for commercial purposes, not for private and domestic use, and that therefore Section 70 did not apply.

EasyInternetcafé was found to be liable on the basis of acts being performed by their employees as part of their duties. In an out of court settlement, EasyInternetcafé agreed to pay the BPI £80,000 in damages for copyright infringement, plus legal costs of £130,000.

Further information

British Phonographic Industries, www.bpi.co.uk (the anti-piracy section of
    their website can be found at www.bpi.co.uk/piracy).
British Phonographic Industries (2006) *Illegal Filesharing Factsheet – Online
    music piracy: the UK record industry's response*,
    www.bpi.co.uk/pdf/Illegal_Filesharing_Factsheet.pdf.
International Federation of the Phonographic Industry (2003) *Copyright Use
    and Security Guide*, www.ifpi.org/content/library/academic-brochure-
    english.pdf.
Madden, Mary and Lenhart, Amanda (2003) *Music Downloading, File Sharing
    and Copyright*, Pew Internet Project.

Notes

1   US District Court, Central Division of California, 10 August 2000. 2000
    B.C. Intell. Prop. & Tech. F. 040401.
2   See *E Commerce Bulletin*, January 2001.

3   BBC Throws Strop at 'Ceefax Google', *The Register*, (1 April 2005), www.theregister.com/2005/04/01/ceefax_google/print.html.

4   *Wiley Sues 10 Illegal Online Resellers*, John Wiley press release, March 2005.

5   For example, media stories on file sharing include:

- (2006) eDonkey Firm to Pay RIAA $30 Million by Nate Mook, *BetaNews*, (12 September).
- (2005) ISPs Ordered to Disclose UK File-sharers' Identities, *Out-Law.com*, (20 April), www.out-law.com/page-5568-theme=default.
- (2007) RIAA Loses Another File-sharing Case, *Electronista.com*, (10 April).
- (2007) Teen Charged with Illegal Filesharing, *Aftenposten*, (4 January).

3

Digital rights management systems

CONTENTS OF CHAPTER 3

3.1 Introduction

Digital rights management is commonly understood to be the generic term for a set of technologies for the identification and protection of intellectual property in digital form. Digital rights management systems comprise two key elements:

- rights management information (RMI)
- technical protection measures (TPMs).

Rights management information identifies digital works and manages the provision of material to customers. RMI also transmits information about the use of the product to the rightsholder. One reason for this would be to enable remuneration to authors.

Technical protection measures enforce the licence terms and may restrict access and use. They prevent unauthorized copying.

In order to make a distinction between these two elements of a digital rights management system, Intellact (in its evidence to the All Party Internet Group's[1] investigation into digital rights management systems) said that rights management information expresses the rightsholders' intent, while technical protection measures ensure that this is honoured.

Digital rights management systems have a set of rules – or a rights model – at their heart. They are all about the management of digital information. They consist of a set of backend processes which are used in order to:

- protect intellectual property rights
- control access to works
- control payment
- control use
- control the integrity of the work.

From the rightsowners' point of view they have obvious benefits, because they can prevent unauthorized duplication of a copyright holder's work, and ensure continued revenue streams. But not everyone sees digital rights management systems in such a positive light. Richard Stallman, for example, came up with his own definition of digital rights management systems: content restriction annulment and protection (or CRAP for short).

3.2 Rights management information

Rights management information is any information provided by the copyright owner which identifies the work, the author or any other rightsholder, information about the terms and conditions of use of the work, and any numbers or codes that represent such information.

There are various ways to identify your copyright-protected material. You may, for example, label the digital content with a copyright notice or a warning label such as 'May be reproduced for non-commercial purposes only'. It is good practice also to include a copyright statement on every page of your business website that spells out the terms and conditions for use of the content on that page.

Any attempt to interfere with this data, remove it or transmit a work without it is an offence. Indeed, it is an offence to knowingly and without authority distribute, import for distribution or communicate to the public copies of a copyright work from which electronic rights management information has been removed or altered without authority, and where the offending party knows, or has reason to believe, that by so doing he is inducing, enabling, facilitating or concealing an infringement of copyright (Section 296ZG, CDPA 1988).

Changing the law to make it an offence to tamper with or remove this information has had the effect of strengthening the author's moral right of paternity. If, for example, there is a statement such as, 'Joe Bloggs has asserted his right under the Copyright, Designs and Patents Act 1988 to be identified as the author of this work', it would be illegal to remove this.

Section 296ZG of the CDPA Electronic rights management information

(1) This section applies where a person (D), knowingly and without authority, removes or alters electronic rights management information which
    (a) is associated with a copy of a copyright work, or
    (b) appears in connection with the communication to the public of a copyright work, and

    where D knows, or has reason to believe, that by so doing he is inducing, enabling, facilitating or concealing an infringement of copyright.

(2) This section also applies where a person (E), knowingly and without authority, distributes, imports for distribution or communicates to the public copies of a copyright work from which electronic rights management information *Continued on next page*

Continued from previous page

    (a) associated with the copies, or

    (b) appearing in connection with the communication to the public of the work

has been removed or altered without authority and where E knows, or has reason to believe, that by so doing he is inducing, enabling, facilitating or concealing an infringement of copyright.

(3) A person issuing to the public copies of, or communicating, the work to the public, has the same rights against D and E as a copyright owner has in respect of an infringement of copyright.

(4) The copyright owner or his exclusive licensee, if he is not the person issuing to the public copies of, or communicating, the work to the public, also has the same rights against D and E as he has in respect of an infringement of copyright.

(5) The rights conferred by subsections (3) and (4) are concurrent, and sections 101(3) and 102(1) to (4) apply, in proceedings under this section, in relation to persons with concurrent rights as they apply, in proceedings mentioned in those provisions, in relation to a copyright owner and exclusive licensee with concurrent rights.

(6) The following provisions apply in relation to proceedings under this section as in relation to proceedings under Part 1 (copyright) –

    (a) sections 104 to 106 of this Act (presumptions as to certain matters relating to copyright); and

    (b) section 72 of the Supreme Court Act 1981, section 15 of the Law Reform (Miscellaneous Provisions) (Scotland) Act 1985 and section 94A of the Judicature (Northern Ireland) Act 1978 (withdrawal of privilege against self-incrimination in certain proceedings relating to intellectual property).

(7) In this section –

    (a) expressions which are defined for the purposes of Part 1 of this Act (copyright) have the same meaning as in that Part; and

    (b) 'rights management information' means any information provided by the copyright owner or the holder of any right under copyright which identifies the work, the author, the copyright owner or the holder of any intellectual property rights, or information about the terms and conditions of use of the work, and any numbers or codes that represent such information.

Electronic copyright management systems (ECMS):

- track and monitor usage (security, authentication)
- licence and charge royalties (payment).

3.3 Technical protection measures

Technical protection measures:

- enforce the licence terms
- are able to restrict access and use
- prevent unauthorized copying.

In order to qualify for protection under the law, technical protection measures must be:

- designed to protect the work
- effective.

It is an offence to circumvent a technical protection measure. This originally derives from the WIPO Copyright Treaty (WCT), which was implemented in Europe through the Copyright Directive (2001/29/EC article 6), which in turn was implemented in the UK through SI 2003/2498.

3.3.1 Technology to control access to digital works

There are a number of mechanisms for controlling access to digital works:

1 Computer operating systems have security and integrity features such as traditional file access privileges.
2 Rights management languages (such as Rights Expression Language) express in machine-readable form the rights and responsibilities of owners, distributors and users, which enables the computer to determine whether requested actions fall within a permitted range.

3   Encryption allows digital works to be scrambled so that they can be unscrambled only by legitimate users. Encryption can be used to scramble content in order to make it unusable by unauthorized users unless they are in possession of the relevant key: the code that can decipher the encrypted message.

4   Persistent encryption permits the buyer to use information while the system maintains it in an encrypted form.

5   Digital watermarks add a small amount of information to the work, which identifies that work and cannot easily be removed. Instead the mark follows the content when it is copied, no matter how the copying occurred. These marks are used by rightsholders who wish to keep track of any copying and distribution of their digital works. Watermarks embed information, such as information about ownership, into a digital work in much the same way that a piece of paper can carry a watermark. Watermarks can be used to guarantee the integrity and authenticity of digital content, and ensure that bootleg copies are unusable. DVDs and CDs can be watermarked. For example, a copied DVD can be recognized as illegal when the watermark does not match the number pressed onto the plastic of a DVD disk.

6   Fingerprinting algorithms take a little piece of the information which identifies the work, although the work itself is not affected.

DRM techniques are not new. The Serial Copy Management System was developed in the 1980s for use on CDs. Using copy control marks, it enabled digital copies to be made from the 'master' copy but not from subsequent copies. Region encoding, the system that prevents DVDs from being viewed in a region other than that in which they were released, has also existed for many years.

3.4 Problems

3.4.1 Restrictions on users' rights

A question which hasn't satisfactorily been resolved is: what if the law entitles you to benefit from a copyright exception – how can you exercise that right[2] if it can only be done by breaking a lock and thereby committing an offence?

The sorts of copyright exception that I am thinking of here would include:

- making a copy for non-commercial research or private study (s.29)
- quoting from a work for the purposes of criticism and review (s.30)
- making a copy for the purposes of news reporting
- making a copy for the conduct of judicial or parliamentary proceedings or a royal commission or other statutory inquiries (ss.45–46).

If the protections which form part of a digital rights management system are applied to the work, any of the permitted acts or exceptions are effectively rendered worthless. Or, to put it another way, the digital rights management system trumps fair dealing.

There is no provision for circumventing a technical protection measure, even for a lawful use. Circumvention of DRM technology is likely to remain illegal, even after the copyright term has expired. However, the Institute for Public Policy Research (IPPR) recommends that anti-circumvention provisions provided in UK law should cease to apply once copyright protection has expired (Davies and Withers, 2006).

In 2003, two new copyright exceptions designed to benefit people with a visual impairment came into force. They allow a copy to be made in a format which is accessible to the visually impaired person, as long as there isn't a commercially available accessible copy. Digital rights management systems cause difficulties for the visually impaired wishing to have a copy in an accessible format such as Braille. Technical protection measures contravene disability discrimination law because they prevent production of accessible copies for the 'print disabled'. The 'read aloud' or 'text to speech' feature within the software (e.g. for Adobe, http://safari.oreilly.com/0321305302/cho71eu1sec4) may, for example, have been disabled. There is no adequate remedy available for visually impaired persons if a DRM system makes it impossible for them to use a product.

Most technical protection measures make copyright perpetual, which goes against the long-standing principles of all existing copyright laws. Technical protection measures are not time limited. Even when copyright material enters the public domain, the TPM does not expire, thereby preventing access to the content. The ownership of the rights may be impossible to trace, rendering the product orphaned, and it is probable that no key would exist to unlock the DRM.

DRMs can be withdrawn yet still lock up the work. For example, one at the British Library with a life of three years has been withdrawn from service, so in three years' time no one will be able to access the content it protects.

3.4.2 Privacy issues

Digital rights management systems do not merely restrict use of copyrighted material in ways already granted by statutory or common law applying to copyright; they can also monitor consumption and user behaviour:

- They invade a sphere with sensitive personal data potentially revealing political convictions, religious or philosophical beliefs, sexual orientation or race.
- The consumer will often be unaware of these monitoring devices or the information that they collect, and will have no control over its use by the DRM controller.
- In the wake of 9/11, anti-terrorism laws are increasingly invading people's privacy, and the information collected by RMI may become accessible to government agencies.
- Such data requires the full protection of data protection legislation.

Further information

Cohen, Julie E. (2003) DRM and Privacy, *Communications of the ACM*, **46** (4), 46–9.

Davies, William and Withers, Kay (2006) *Public Innovation: intellectual property in a digital age*, Institute for Public Policy Research.

3.5 Trusted intermediaries

Librarians and archivists should be subject to a new exception making them trusted intermediaries, thereby enabling them to circumvent TPMs and/or require publishers to give libraries and archives clean digital copies or the key to TPMs. Then they would be able to:

- make copies which are permitted under statutory exceptions and limitations to copyright or database right, including accessible copies for print-disabled people; and
- migrate content to different platforms and formats in order to continue to make it accessible and to preserve it in digital form. Libraries need to retain access to content in perpetuity where they have a remit to preserve our cultural heritage.

3.6 Labelling

When consumers purchase an electronic product such as an e-book or a DVD, it is only fair that they know precisely what it is that they are buying. They should be made aware of any limitations or restrictions on the usage of the item resulting from the use of technical protection measures. In some countries, labelling laws have been used to address this issue.

Recommendation 16 of the Gowers Report says that the Department of Trade and Industry (DTI) should investigate the possibility of providing consumer guidance on DRM systems through a labelling convention without imposing unnecessary regulatory burdens.

3.7 Complaints procedure

Article 6(4) of the Copyright Directive says that:

> ... in the absence of voluntary measures taken by rightholders including agreements between rightholders and other parties concerned, Member States shall take appropriate measures to ensure that rightholders make available to the beneficiary of an exception or limitation provided for in national law ... the means of benefiting from that exception or limitation, to the

extent necessary to benefit from that exception or limitation and where that beneficiary has legal access to the protected work or subject matter concerned.

It is clear that this only applies if there is no licensing scheme in place to cover the category of the material in question, and also that it does not cover material available 'on demand'. CDPA 1988 Section 296ZE says: 'this section does not apply to copyright works made available to the public on agreed contractual terms in such a way that members of the public may access them from a place and at a time individually chosen by them.'

UK law states that citizens can complain to the Secretary of State for Trade and Industry if they feel that their fair dealing rights have been limited by a DRM system. However, this does not apply to 'on demand' content – that is, to works which have been 'made available to the public on agreed contractual terms in such a way that members of the public may access them from a place and time individually chosen by them'.

Where someone issues a 'notice of complaint' to the Secretary of State, then (if it is appropriate) the Secretary of State issues directions to the rightsowner to ensure that the permitted act can occur. However, if these directions are ignored then it would be necessary for the complainant to take action for breach of statutory duty. This fails to meet the users' need for timely access to works and inspires little faith because:

- An order made by the Secretary of State can be ignored by the content provider – the government can only name and shame.
- The onus is put on the user to seek judicial redress through the courts if the rightsowner fails to comply with an instruction from the Secretary of State following a ruling in favour of the applicant.
- It is likely to be both time-consuming and expensive to the complainant.
- Even though this provision was introduced in October 2003, the UK's Intellectual Property Office hasn't introduced any complaints procedure.
- The vagueness of the process serves to stifle complaints.

A major difficulty for individuals wishing to enforce their rights through the courts is the level of risk involved in taking such a course of action, given the rule that the loser pays the costs of the winning side. This means that justice is beyond the reach of individuals because they can seldom afford to gamble that their case is so strong as to guarantee a win – and to lose would imperil their savings, and perhaps even their homes.

3.8 Interoperability

Songs purchased from a legitimate download service don't necessarily play on all hardware; and this raises the question of interoperability. Should governments force digital music companies to use a single, unified DRM system, in order to allow songs purchased from any download service to run on any hardware?

The House of Congress Judiciary Committee's Subcommittee on Courts, the Internet and Intellectual Property looked at this issue. The Committee asked four industry representatives to testify on the issue of proprietary DRM schemes, which can prevent a downloaded track from being played on a player such as an iPod, unless the song is downloaded in an unregulated MP3 format. Each of the four speakers advocated a market-driven response, instead of government intervention. Several speakers specifically cited the landmark fight between VHS and Betamax videocassette standards, which was ultimately decided by the marketplace, and not regulators or the courts.

The International Digital Media Project (www.dmpf.org) is an international forum aimed at standardizing digital media and copy protection technologies. The initiative brings together more than 25 member companies across the digital content and device industries including Panasonic, Mitsubishi Electric Corp., Telecom Italia and the BBC. By working towards interoperable DRM, the Digital Media Project believes that a larger market will be created for everyone in the industry, to the benefit of content creators, distributors and device makers – but more importantly it will be acceptable to end users.

➡ Relevant legal cases
Lexmark v Static Control Components

Lexmark had put computer chips into their printer cartridges, which had the effect of making it difficult if not impossible for people to use low-cost refill cartridges from rival players in the toner cartridge industry.

Lexmark took legal action with a view to getting Static Control Components, a maker of microchips used in replacement laser printer cartridges, to stop making and selling products which could be used in Lexmark printers. In 2002 Lexmark sued Static Control, claiming that their Smartek chips, which can be used in toner cartridges developed by Lexmark, violate the Digital Millenium Copyright Act, which makes it an offence to circumvent technical measures that restrict access to copyrighted works.

In October 2004, overturning a lower court decision, the Sixth Circuit Court of Appeals ruled to the effect that Lexmark could not leverage copyright and use the DMCA provisions on technical protection measures in order to keep a competitor from making toner cartridges that work with Lexmark printers.

In February 2006, United States District Court judge Karl Forester ruled that Static Control's manufacture, distribution and sales of its microchips for use with Lexmark printers did not violate the DMCA.

In a similar case, Hewlett-Packard Corporation was sued for allegedly including computer chips in their printer cartridges which instruct the cartridges to stop working on a pre-determined date even if they still contain ink.

In an article dating back to 2003 Wendy Seltzer, speaking for the Electronic Frontier Foundation, said that 'the Lexmark lawsuit shows how far copyright law has strayed from its original foundations' (Bray, 2003).

Remanufacturers have about 25% of the toner cartridge market, according to industry estimates. If they are blocked from reproducing computer chips, they obviously won't be able to offer low-cost alternatives.

DVD protection violates consumer rights, says French court

The Paris Court of Appeal ruled that digital rights management software on a DVD breached the rights of a purchaser who wanted to copy the film onto video for his own personal use.[3]

Sony BMG incident

Sony BMG shipped millions of CDs in the USA which contained two extremely problematic copy protection systems. One system, called MediaMax, installed itself even if a user refused permission and hid its device driver from standard tools. The other, XCPP, contained what was rather loosely called a 'rootkit'. In addition to their copy protection role, both systems contacted a website whenever the user inserted a protected disc, even though this constituted a gross intrusion of privacy. When this came to light, and users complained, the company further compounded the problem by releasing a flawed un-install system (that compromised the security of those who ran it). It eventually settled out of court in the face of a number of class-action lawsuits. The settlement promised up to $175 to consumers in California who provided documentation relating to the damage they said had been done to their computers. On top of that the company was required to pay $750,000 to the attorneys general in fines and to pay legal fees.[4]

At the time of writing Sony BMG are trying to recoup their losses by suing the company responsible for the technology, namely the Amergence Group. The case was filed in a New York state court at the beginning of July 2007. Amergence is accused of offering Sony software that didn't work as promised, negligence and unfair business practices.

3.9 APIG Inquiry and Gowers Review

In 2006 the All Party Internet Group published the findings of its inquiry into digital rights management.[5] These findings were taken into account by the Gowers Review, although the Gowers Review made very limited comments regarding the implications of digital rights management systems.

The key recommendations of the APIG inquiry were:

- The Office of Fair Trading (OFT) should bring forward appropriate labelling regulations so that it will become crystal clear to consumers what they will and will not be able to do with digital content that they purchase.
- OFCOM should publish guidance to make it clear that companies distributing TPM systems in the UK would, if they have features such as those in Sony-BMG's MediaMax and XCP systems, run a significant risk of being prosecuted for criminal actions.
- The Department of Trade and Industry should investigate the single-market issues raised during the Inquiry, with a view to addressing them at the European level.
- The government should not legislate to make DRM systems mandatory.
- The Department for Culture, Media and Sport should review the level of funding for pilot projects that address access to e-books by those with visual disabilities, and action should be taken if they are failing to achieve positive results.
- The Department of Trade and Industry should revisit the results of its review into its moribund 'IP Advisory Committee' and reconstitute it as several more focused forums; one of these should be a 'UK Stakeholders Group' to be chaired by the British Library.
- The government should consider granting a much wider-ranging exemption to the anti-circumvention measures in the 1988 Copyright, Designs and Patents Act for genuine academic research.
- The Department for Culture, Media and Sport should hold a formal public consultation, not only on the technical details but also on the general principles that have been established.

There are two recommendations in the Gowers Review which relate to digital rights management systems:

- Recommendation 15: make it easier for users to file notices of complaints relating to DRM tools by providing an accessible web interface on the Patent Office website by 2008.

- Recommendation 16: the DTI should investigate the possibility of providing consumer guidance on DRM systems through a labelling convention without imposing unnecessary regulatory burdens.

3.10 Legislation

The main pieces of legislation relevant to DRM systems are:

- WIPO Copyright Treaty 1996 (WCT)
- The 'Infosoc' Directive 2001/29/EC
- The Copyright and Related Rights Regulations 2003
- The Copyright, Designs and Patents Act 1988 as amended.

Articles 6 (obligations as to technical measures) and 7 (obligations concerning rights-management information) of the Copyright Directive (2001/29/EC) provide a whole new set of tools which help to protect the interests of rightsholders. If a user breaks those locks, then they commit an offence (whether civil or criminal).

Article 6.4 of Directive 2001/29/EC says:

. . . in the absence of voluntary measures taken by rightsholders, including agreements between rightsholders and other parties concerned, Member States shall take appropriate measures to ensure that rightsholders make available to the beneficiary of an exception or limitation provided for in national law in accordance with Article 5(2)(a), 2(c), 2(d), 2(e), 3(a), 3(b) or 3(e) the means of benefiting from that exception or limitation, to the extent necessary to benefit from that exception or limitation and where the beneficiary has legal access to the protected work or subject-matter concerned.

Section 296ZE of the CDPA 1988 covers the remedy where effective technical measures prevent permitted acts:

This section does not apply to copyright works made available to the public on agreed contractual terms in such a way that members of the public may access them from a place and at a time individually chosen by them.

In the UK, licences and contract trump copyright law, and can override fair dealing exceptions (see Chapter 6.2). In a British Library survey, out of 30 licences surveyed at random the vast majority did not give provisions as generous as those that would be provided under fair dealing or library privilege in copyright law. Restrictions included limiting the extent of material that could be copied: one licence stated that 'misuse includes . . . reproducing in any way copyright material' – a clear barrier to conducting research or criticizing works (British Library, 2006).

The British Library has urged that it should be supplied with DRM-free copies of digital works, once digital deposit begins in earnest. IPPR recommends that this should be a feature of digital deposit regulations, and urges content providers to respect the value of libraries' activities in this area.

Further information

All Party Internet Group (2006) *Digital Rights Management: report of an inquiry by the All Party Internet Group*, www.apcomms.org.uk/apig/current-activities/apig-inquiry-into-digital-rights-management.html.

Bray, Hiawatha (2003) N. C. Printer Cartridges Maker is Allowed to Design Lexmark-like Products, *Boston Globe*, (30 October).

British Library (2006) Response to Gowers, www.hm-treasury.gov.uk/media/5/6/british_library_ 375_132kb.pdf

Intrallect (2004) *Digital Rights Management: final report*, www.intrallect.com/index.php/intrallect/knowledge_base/general_articles/jisc_drm_study_2004__1.

IPR Helpdesk (2004) *Digital Rights Management Systems*, IPR Helpdesk.

Notes

1 *Digital Rights Management: report of an inquiry by the All Party Internet Group*, (2006), www.appcomms.org.uk/apig/current-activities/apig-inquiry-into-digital-rights-management.html.

2 The use of the word 'right' is misleading. There is no right of fair dealing, for example. It is merely a defence which you would use in court if you were accused of copyright infringement. The problem is that fair dealing

isn't well defined within our copyright legislation, and therefore it is impossible for a DRM system to enforce.

3   See www.out-law.com/default.aspx?page=5615.

4   See Sony BMG Settles 'Rootkit' Case, *Out-law News*, 20 December 2006, www.out-law.com/page-7596.

5   See www.apcomms.org.uk/apig/current-activities/apig-inquiry-into-digital-rights-management.html.

4

Orphan works

4.1 The problem of orphan works

'Orphan works' is the term that has come to be used to describe works where the rightsholder is difficult or even impossible to identify or locate.

Libraries, researchers, archives and museums often want to republish 'orphan' works for archival, research and preservation purposes. However, orphan works cause huge problems for rights clearances – they are still in copyright, but their rightsowners remain untraceable after reasonable enquiry. Libraries, archives, museums and galleries can often spend a significant amount of their scarce resources trying to trace rightsowners in order to clear rights.

When people wish to make use of a work that is protected by copyright, and that use would not be covered by one of the copyright exceptions or permitted acts, the permission of the copyright holder is required. Such a requirement is perfectly understandable. However, this can be a real problem when a library has undertaken a reasonable search for the copyright owner but the rightsowner still cannot be located, because if at that stage they do decide to go ahead with the copying, they are taking a risk. Indeed, the risk of liability for copyright infringement is enough to prevent many stakeholders from making use of a work.

In evidence to the Gowers Review of Intellectual Property, the National Council on Archives (NCA) told of the following:

> A local historian published a book with photographs all of which he had permission to use except for one, for which he was unable to find the copyright owner, although he spent considerable effort in his search. Deciding to go ahead without permission he had the book printed with the usual calls for the owner. Immediately the copyright owner demanded £20,000 for using his photograph without permission. The local historian had to pay a much smaller payment but had to pay.[1]

It seems unfair if a diligent – but unsuccessful – search for the rightsowner has been undertaken, yet subsequent use of a copyright work results in unreasonable demands for recompense or possibly in litigation.

The problem of orphan works jeopardizes the principal role of libraries in preserving the world's cultural heritage and in making it accessible. The most effective and often the only possible way of making works accessible is to digitize them. However, in creating digital collections libraries often have to go to great lengths and incur significant costs in order to ensure that they are not breaking copyright law.

In a review of the body of European Community law on copyright and related rights, the Institute for Information Law (IViR) at the University of Amsterdam (2006) states: '[T]his is indeed a case of structural market failure that would justify some form of legislative intervention, even though the size of the problem is as yet difficult to quantify.'

Although the IViR report maintains that it is difficult to quantify the problem, the Gowers Review does provide some assistance here. Indeed, one of the most noteworthy points about the Gowers Review is the way in which it is very much evidence-based. The final report[2] cites a number of statistics which do help us to get an idea of the scale of the problem posed by orphan works:

- It is estimated that only 2% of all works protected by copyright are commercially available.
- In 1930 there were 10,027 books published in the USA, but by 2001 all but 174 of these were out of print.
- The British Library estimates that 40% of all print works are orphan works.
- In a British Library study to get permission to digitize 200 sound recordings, researchers were unable to identify the rightsholders for almost half the recordings.

It can prove to be impossible to locate the rightsowner for a number of reasons. They include the following:

- There is no information about the author on the work itself (for example, on a photograph); books and journals will normally have ISBNs and ISSNs respectively (unless they were published before this system was introduced), but for some types of material there won't be any markings along similar lines.
- The term is dependent on the date of the death of the author, but it it isn't always easy to find out when an author died, and therefore to know when the work comes out of copyright protection.
- The author is known, but has died, and there is no information about his or her heirs.
- The company which held the copyright no longer exists; indeed, the Gowers Report uses the word 'abandonware' to describe the situation when businesses go bankrupt or merge, and information about copyright ownership gets lost.
- The author is no longer the rightsowner.

Orphan works present a problem when people try to undertake digitization projects, or to publish historical letters, sound recordings, film footage, etc. The problem of orphan works can affect all types of works, and is especially problematic when it comes to works with multiple ownership. Problems arise through the administrative burden posed, the amount of time required and the cost involved.

Every time the duration of copyright protection has been extended, the difficulties involved in locating rightsholders and obtaining permission for older works has increased. The fewer works there are in the public domain, the more works there are that require permission. When the term of copyright protection has been increased, this has exacerbated the problem by increasing the number of orphan works. Thankfully, Recommendation 4 in the Gowers Review states: 'Policy makers should adopt the principle that the term and scope of protection for IP rights should not be altered retrospectively.'

People are often willing to pay for copyright permission, but where orphan works are concerned, they are put off by the high cost involved in finding the rightsowner.

What do you do if the copyright owner:

- cannot be identified
- has been identified, but can't be located
- doesn't respond to your request
- is uncertain about the ownership of the rights (for example, the publisher cannot find the written copyright assignment)?

The options available in such circumstances are as follows:

- Don't digitize the material under any circumstances.
- Digitize the content but continue to make efforts to find the owners.
- Include a disclaimer in the material that you digitize.
- Take out indemnity insurance.

However, there are risks associated with several of these options. As most of the key terms in copyright law (such as 'substantial', 'reasonable', 'fair dealing' or 'commercial purpose') are not clearly defined, copyright compliance becomes a matter of risk management.

Some copyright experts have argued that it should become an offence to make an unjustifiable threat of infringement proceedings, as is the case in other areas of intellectual property law. The wording of Section 70 of the Patents Act 1977 could, for example, be used by replacing the words 'a patent' with 'copyright' throughout, and also completely deleting the wording in Sections 70(2)(b) and 70(4) of the Patents Act.

> Patents Act 1977 s70 – Remedy for groundless threats of infringement proceedings
> (1) Where a person (whether or not the proprietor of, or entitled to any right in, a patent) by circulars, advertisements or otherwise threatens another person with proceedings for any infringement of a patent, a person aggrieved by the threats (whether or not he is the person to whom the threats are made) may ... bring proceedings in the court against the person making the threats.

In order to obtain the support of both the users and the owners of rights, any legislative solution to the orphan works problem needs to balance their respective interests. The user wants legal certainty about his or her liability exposure in the event that the rightsowner might surface in the future, while the rightsowner wants to be able to recover compensation for the use of his or her work, and to be able to prevent further use of the work.

4.2 The international perspective
4.2.1 Canada

Under Canadian copyright law, the Copyright Board of Canada is authorized to grant a licence to use an orphan work.[3] An application must be submitted in writing and contain considerable detail: the applicant must describe the work that he or she wishes to use and explain how, when or for how long it will be used. He or she must report in detail on the efforts taken to locate the copyright owner. When all the required information has been received, the Board determines on a case-by-case basis, within 30–45 days, whether the applicant has made every reasonable effort to identify the copyright holder. When the licence is granted, it sets the terms and conditions in relation to permitted use. Furthermore, it determines the royalty fees which have to be paid to the copyright collecting society that would normally represent the unlocatable copyright owner. The copyright collecting society has to reimburse the person who establishes, within five years of the expiry of the licence, ownership of the copyright of the work covered by the licence. The Canadian system deals only with known but unlocatable copyright owners; it does not deal with unknown copyright owners.

The Canadian system has not been extensively used. Since the provisions were enacted in 1990, only 192 such licences have been issued (an average around a dozen per year). Six applications have been denied, although three of these were because they related to unpublished works and thus were not covered by the Canadian legislation.

4.2.2 Denmark

Danish copyright law allows exploitation of works if reasonable efforts have been made to clear the rights but the rightsholders cannot be traced. The Danish model consists of a system of extended collective licensing; this licensing regime has been adopted by several Nordic governments. Once an organization represents a large enough number of copyright owners from a particular sector, its authority to license is 'extended' thereby allowing it to license the works of all of the copyright owners in that sector, including non-member nationals and foreign copyright owners. This allows the user to obtain a licence from a collecting agency without having to locate the rightsholder. Licenses are issued in certain cases of non-commercial use of orphan works: for example, copies for the purpose of educational activities, copies for internal use, and reproductions by libraries or by governmental or municipal institutions and other social or non-profit institutions for the use of visually handicapped and hearing-impaired persons. Such licences require the remuneration of the author in the event s/he is identified.

4.2.3 France

The French society of authors is creating a database of deceased authors, and the French user community is seeking legislation to indemnify users if the deceased author is not on this register (LACA and the Museums Copyright Group, 2006, 23).

4.2.4 USA

In January 2006, the US Copyright Office published a report on orphan works which examined the extent of the problem and outlined potential solutions. The system the Office preferred was one of limited liability. This means that users of orphan works are still infringing copyright. However, if they have conducted a 'reasonable search' they cannot be sued for infringement if the owner subsequently emerges. The copyright owner will be eligible to receive remuneration from the user of the orphan work: the fee would represent a proportion of the value generated by commercial uses of the work. The user would then have to negotiate a fee for any continued use of the work. For non-commercial uses of the work, the owner will be able to request that the work is no longer used and, if the user complies, no remuneration is necessary, but they will also be able to negotiate terms for continued use.

In May 2006 a bill was introduced in the 2nd session of the 109th Congress with the short title 'Orphan Works Act of 2006' (H.R. 5439). This subsequently became part of H.R. 6052, the 'Copyright Modernization Act of 2006'. However, the proposed legislation was eventually withdrawn.

4.2.5 UK

The Gowers Review made three recommendations relating to orphan works:

- Recommendation 13: a provision for orphan works should be proposed to the European Commission, amending Directive 2001/29/EC, as Article 5 of this directive sets out the permissible exceptions to copyright and none of these seem to envisage a commercial orphan works exception.
- Recommendation 14a: the Patent Office should issue clear guidance on the parameters of a 'reasonable search' for orphan works, in consultation with rightsholders, collecting societies, rightsowners and archives, when an orphan works exception comes into being.

- Recommendation 14b: the Patent Office should establish a voluntary register of copyright, either on its own or through partnerships with database holders, by 2008.

Several points of clarification are worth making about these recommendations.

Article 5 of the Copyright Directive (2001/29/EC) sets out the range of copyright exceptions available to EU member states. This is an exhaustive list from which any member state can select the exceptions they want to make use of, but member states are not able to add to that list. Article 5 also uses a form of words which is substantially the same as that found in the Berne three-step test; any copyright exception within a member state of the European Union has to meet those three tests (see Chapter 2.5). None of the exceptions in Article 5 as they currently stand would seem to cater for orphan works.

It is clear from the Gowers Review and from what we can learn from developments internationally that the user of an orphan work would need to carry out a diligent search for the copyright owner. A key element of any orphan works solution would be the precise parameters of a 'reasonable search'. There are several places in the CDPA 1988 where 'reasonable inquiry' is given as a requirement before using a work beyond the limits allowed under the Act.[4]

With regard to the Gowers recommendation about setting up a voluntary register, it is worth noting that it would have to be voluntary because under the Berne Convention copyright protection is given without any formality. Thus a compulsory register would contravene the Convention by making copyright protection dependent on a statutory registration process.

The UK Intellectual Property Office's *Review of the Copyright Tribunal* (2007) states that the Copyright Tribunal should be responsible for granting licences for the use of orphan works.

4.3 Proposals to solve the problem

In a review of the copyright acquis,[5] Berndt Hugenholz runs through a number of options for solving the orphan works problem:

- Make copyright ownership or rights management information publicly accessible.
- Implement a system of collective rights management whereby rights management organizations are entitled to grant licences that include even those works the rightsowners of which cannot be traced by reasonable means.
- Encourage users to apply to a representative private organization to obtain an indemnity or security.
- Set up a competent public authority to issue a non-exclusive licence for the use of orphan works.
- Introduce an exception or limitation permitting the re-utilization of orphan works under certain conditions.
- Implement a liability rule for bona fide re-utilization by users who undertake reasonable steps (to limit the liability).

One organization, representing the makers of watermarking software, has published a white paper which says that the US government should make it a requirement of any use of a copyright work to check to see if it contains ownership information in the metadata. My concern with such a proposal is that ownership can change over a period of time, and I wonder whether the watermark software would be updated in order to reflect any changes in ownership of the rights.

There is a desire to develop a European Digital Library; it may seem ironic that the EU is having to work out how it can digitize content given the highly restrictive copyright laws whose introduction it has overseen. The Council of the European Union (2006) has made a commitment to address framework conditions by proposing solutions to certain specific rights issues, such as orphan and out-of-print works, while fully respecting content owners' interests and rights, and ensuring effectiveness in a cross-border context.

Further information

British Screen Advisory Council (2006) *Copyright and Orphan Works: a paper prepared for the Gowers Review*, www.bsac.uk.com/reports/ orphanworkspaper.pdf.

Council of the European Union (2006) *Council Conclusions on the Digitisation and Online Accessiblitiy of Cultural Material, and Digital Preservation* C297/01,
http://ec.europa.eu/information_society/activities/digital_libraries/doc/ culture_council/council_conclusions_nov_2006.pdf.

Institute for Information Law, University of Amsterdam (2006) *The Recasting of Copyright and Related Rights for the Knowledge Economy*,
www.openrightsgroup.org/orgwiki/index.php.

Libraries and Archives Copyright Alliance and the Museums Copyright Group (2006) *Joint Proposals to the UK Government for Revisions to the Copyright Designs and Patents Act 1988*, CILIP,
www.cilip.org.uk/NR/rdonlyres/D7C128B7-896C-49F5-AE27-E549DB415B2D/0/LACA_MCGProposalsCDPA_revFINAL_21apr06.pdf.

Open Rights Group, www.openrightsgroup.org.

STM (2006) *STM Position: the use of orphan works*, www.stm-assoc.org.

UK Intellectual Property Office (2007) *Review of the Copyright Tribunal*, UK IPO.

US Copyright Office (2006) *Report on Orphan Works*,
www.copyright.gov/orphan/orphan-report-full.pdf.

Notes

1   See www.ncaonline.org.uk/materials/nca_gowers.pdf.

2   See p. 69 of the Gowers Review, www.hm-treasury.gov.uk/independent_ reviews/gowers_review_intellectual_property/gowersreview_index.cfm.

3   For further information see the *Unlocatable Copyright Owners* page of the Copyright Board of Canada website, www.cb-cda.gc.ca/unlocatable/index-e.html.

4   See Section 41(2) Copying by librarians: supply of copies to other libraries, and Section 57(1) Anonymous or pseudonymous works: acts permitted on assumptions as to expiry of copyright or death of author.

5   Berndt Hugenholz review of the acquis 'The recasting of copyright and related rights for the knowledge economy', IViR, November 2006, Chapter 5.

5

Permitted acts

5.1　Digital content and the copyright exceptions

An inevitable question arises with regard to the copyright exceptions: do they apply to digital content?

By way of background, it is worth mentioning again the Berne three-step test. The Berne Convention of 1886 enabled national legislatures to provide a number of copyright exceptions or permitted acts, as long as they met a three-step test. Exceptions only apply:

- in certain special cases
- if they do not conflict with a normal exploitation of the work or other subject matter
- if they do not unreasonably prejudice the legitimate interests of the rightsholder.

A substantially similar form of words is used in Article 5(5) of the Copyright Directive 2001/29/EC. In consequence, any copyright exceptions or permitted acts within UK copyright law must comply with the Berne three-step test.

Each exception can only apply in certain special cases. In other words, an exception must be narrowly defined. The wording of each of the exceptions must be looked at carefully. For example, the exceptions in Section 31A and B of the CDPA 1988, which relate to the making of an accessible copy for a visually impaired person, do extend to digital content, but with certain constraints. Both the 'one for one' exception and the 'multiple copy' exception (see 5.3 below) do not apply:

- if the master copy is of a musical work, or part of a musical work, and the making of an accessible copy would involve recording a performance of the work or part of it
- if the master copy is of a database, or part of a database, and the making of an accessible copy would infringe copyright in the database.

The provisions of Article 10[1] of the 1996 WIPO Copyright Treaty (WCT), permit contracting parties to carry forward and appropriately extend into the digital environment limitations and exceptions in their national laws which have been considered acceptable under the Berne Convention. Similarly, these provisions permit contracting parties to devise new exceptions and limitations that are appropriate in the digital network environment. Article 10(2) neither reduces nor extends the scope of applicability of the limitations and exceptions permitted by the Berne Convention.

Rightsholders are likely to become particularly nervous or wary when their content is digitized. This is because of the ease with which electronic content can be copied, the quality of the copy, the speed with which copies can be made and the ease with which any copy can be distributed to multiple users.

In the Copyright, Designs and Patents Act 1988, the fair dealing exceptions are not set out in a clear and unambiguous way. The legislation does not make it absolutely clear what would be deemed to be 'fair'. Consequently, this has to be judged on the basis of each individual instance of copying, and no one can be sure that the copying is fair unless it is deemed to be so by a court. Fair dealing is therefore a rather risky and unpredictable defence. In the digital environment rightsholders are particularly keen to protect their intellectual property rights, and in that sense the risks are even higher.

It should be pointed out that fair dealing is not a right, and as such it does not provide any guarantee of immunity against an action for copyright infringement. Rather, it is a defence that you might call upon if you were to be faced with an action for infringement. In such a case, you would have to prove that your copying passed the Berne three-step test.

5.2 Scanning

There may be some limited instances under the copyright exceptions where scanning is permitted, such as the exception relating to fair dealing for non-commercial research or private study. However, it is important to bear in mind that the copyright exceptions are limited in scope, and are not some sort of blanket permission to copy a work.

Scanning and the fair dealing exception for research or private study

The fair dealing exception:

- does not permit communication of the work to the public
- does not permit multiple copying
- does not cover any copies which are made for a commercial purpose.

Thus scanned copies:

- should be within the 'safe' copying limits (see the CILIP coyright posters, www.cilip.org.uk/professionalguidance/copyright/formsandposters/posters.htm.
- shouldn't be put onto a shared drive, computer network or intranet, sent out as an e-mail attachment, or put on a discussion list or a website (all of which would constitute the equivalent of multiple copying).

5.3 Digital information and visually impaired persons

The Copyright (Visually Impaired Persons) Act 2002 came into force in October 2003 and introduced two new copyright exceptions or permitted acts:

1   The 'one for one' exception (CDPA s.31A) states that a visually impaired person can make (or ask anyone to make for them) a single accessible copy of a copyright work for their personal use, subject to a number of conditions. For example, they must have lawful possession of, or be able lawfully to use, an inaccessible copy of the copyright work and a copy that is accessible must not be commercially available. 'Lawful use' would include an item held in a library that they are eligible to use. However, it is important to point out that they cannot keep the accessible copy if they no longer have access to the inaccessible copy. Most of the copyright exceptions only permit a limited amount of the work to be copied, but in this particular instance the whole of the work may be copied and it can be either a published or unpublished work, so this applies to archival collections as well as to libraries.

2   **Under** the 'multiple copy' exception (CDPA 1988 s.31B) educational establishments or bodies not conducted for profit may make multiple accessible copies of a copyright work and supply them to visually impaired people for their personal use, subject to a number of conditions. Within a reasonable time of making these accessible copies, copyright owners must be notified of activity under the exception. Where copyright owners have established a licensing scheme covering the activity that would otherwise be permitted under the exception and have notified the DTI (now the Department for Innovation, Universities and Skills, or DIUS) of the licensing scheme, then licences under that scheme must be taken out. There are currently two such licensing schemes: the Copyright Licensing Agency has one which covers books and journals, and the Music Publishers Association has one which covers sheet music.

There are a number of points to bear in mind regarding both of the exceptions for visually impaired persons. Accessible copies may not be supplied to anyone who can access a commercially available copy. In addition, the exceptions apply to commercially published literary, dramatic, musical and artistic works and published editions. This would include books, journals, newspapers, instruction booklets, manuals, advertisements, maps and knitting patterns, but does not cover databases.

An accessible copy made for a visually impaired person can take any form and so can, for example, be in Braille or Moon, in large print, an audio recording or an electronic copy. However, where an electronic copy is made, those making and using this will need to take particular care to ensure that it is handled appropriately given the ease with which it could be used illegally in ways falling outside the scope of the exceptions.

An accessible copy would be treated as an infringing copy if it is dealt with, and a copyright owner can seek a court order for delivery up of any infringing copies. 'Dealt with' means sold, let for hire, offered or exposed for sale or hire or communicated to the public by electronic means. The last of these would include putting the accessible copy on a website. This would in any case be an illegal activity, unless carried out with the permission of the copyright owner, and so would infringe copyright. Indeed, it could amount to a criminal offence. Anyone found putting accessible copies onto a website without permission could be sued by the copyright owner, who might seek substantial compensation for any damage caused.

The Copyright (Educational Establishments) Order 2005 (SI 2005/223), which was made under Section 174(1)(b) of the CDPA 1988, lists those educational establishments that can take advantage of the copyright exception and make multiple copies for visually impaired persons.

Revealweb (www.revealweb.org.uk), launched in September 2003, provides a catalogue of materials in accessible formats and a database of suppliers (holders, producers and sellers) of accessible formats in the UK.

5.3.1 Concerns over technical protection measures

The use by rightsholders of digital rights management systems to protect their works is a concern for those with a visual impairment, because the ability of the rightsholders to 'lock digital doors' prevents the visually impaired exercising their right to make an accessible copy. The Copyright (Visually Impaired Persons) Act 2002 does not address the problem.

Further information

Higher Education Funding Council for England (2003) *Intellectual Property Rights in E-learning Programmes*, HEFCE.

IFLA (2004) *Limitations and Exceptions to Copyright and Neighbouring Rights in the Digital Environment*, www.ifla.org/III/clm/p1/ilp.htm.

Joint Information Systems Committee/Publishers Association (1998) *Guidelines for Fair Dealing in an Electronic Environment*, JISC/PA.

Note

1   See www.wipo.int/treaties/en/ip/wct/trtdocs_wo033.html#P83_10885 or www.wipo.int/treaties/en/ip/wct/statements.html.

6

Licences, contracts or sets of terms and conditions

6.1 Introduction

The digitization of content is changing the way in which rightsholders protect their intellectual property rights. Instead of relying primarily on copyright law, rightsholders are looking to the use of licences and contracts in order to manage and protect their content.

According to the World Intellectual Property Organization (2003):

licensing implies at least a minimum level of bargaining between the rightsholder and the person who wishes to use the work in a manner covered by the exclusive rights. Even assuming that the terms of use and the royalty are totally standardized, at the very least there is a need to conclude an agreement between the user and the rightsholder or its representative.

However, in practice, there are certain types of agreement which don't provide an opportunity for negotiation. There is a question over the enforceability of agreements of this kind. Examples include:

- shrink-wrap agreements
- click-use agreements
- terms and conditions notices on websites.

Information professionals have to negotiate licence agreements with suppliers on behalf of their organizations in order to set up access to electronic products.

When a supplier sends through a contract for signature, it should be read carefully. If anything in the contract is unclear, clarification should be sought. When a contract for signature is received, it should not be regarded as being set in stone. Instead, receipt of the contract should be regarded as the beginning of a process in which the information professional has the opportunity to negotiate the terms of the agreement.

Licences are contracts that bind both parties to a specific set of terms and conditions. They are governed by the law of contract, and enable information professionals to reach agreement with rightsholders to permit their users to have access to electronic information services in ways that meet their users' needs. The licence agreement defines the material or product to be licensed and specifies how the material can be used, at what price, and for how long.

6.1.1 Shift from 'ownership' to 'leasing'

In the print world there is what is known in the USA as the 'first sale doctrine'. Under this doctrine, when someone buys a book or purchases an issue of a journal, the item is theirs to do with as they wish. They don't own the intellectual property rights to the content, but they do own the physical goods. This entitles them to lend the work to anyone they wish, to sell it second-hand or to access its contents at any time they so choose.

The electronic world operates very differently. It is important to point out that a licence does not confer ownership rights. It merely provides access for a limited period of time to the content being licensed. The licence specifies the conditions under which databases and other copyright works can be used and exploited, and by whom. Typically, the licences that information professionals negotiate are non-exclusive, granting the same rights to many different users. The customer or licensee is merely paying for the privilege of being able to use the information product or service for a limited period of time. In the case of a product containing electronic journals, for example, once the licence comes to an end the customer not only ceases to have access to the current issues of the e-journal(s), he or she also no longer has access to the back issues – unless there is a clause in the agreement covering perpetual access. Indeed, many licence agreements require the licensee to agree to delete any materials that have been downloaded from the product on termination of the contract.

6.2 The relationship between copyright and contract law

Electronic products are often accompanied by a set of terms and conditions, a licence or a contractual agreement. It is important to take on board the implications of this: contracts can override copyright law with very few exceptions. The basic principle is that a contract freely entered into by an adult is legally binding.

Anyone who imagines that the courts will overturn what to them appears to be an unfair contract term needs to think again. In very limited cases where a clause excludes liability, and this is unreasonable and the clause is not negotiated, the courts may overturn it. It will cost the buyer a fortune in legal fees, and they may not win. The courts do not act as a kind of nanny for the businessperson who suddenly realizes that they have inadvertently accepted terms and conditions they should not have.

Under the Unfair Contract Terms Act 1977, a person cannot exclude or restrict his liability for death or personal injury resulting from negligence. He can exclude or restrict liability for other loss or damage resulting from negligence only if the exclusion clauses satisfy a test of reasonableness. It would be for the party seeking to impose a contract term to demonstrate to the court that it was reasonable, should they be challenged.

The Unfair Terms in Consumer Contracts Regulations 1999 (SI 1999/ 2083) state that a term which has not been individually negotiated in a consumer contract is unfair if, contrary to the requirement of good faith, it causes a significant imbalance in the rights and obligations of the parties to the detriment of the consumer.

In a Court of Appeal ruling in 2001, Lord Justice Chadwick said that the courts should be reluctant to interfere in contractual relationships where each party has freely entered into a contract and where each party enjoys reasonably equal bargaining power:

> Where experienced businessmen representing substantial companies of equal bargaining power negotiate an agreement, they may be taken to have had regard to the matters known to them. They should, in my view, be taken to be the best judge of the commercial fairness of the agreement which they have made; including the fairness of each of the terms in that agreement. They should be taken to be the best judge on the question whether the terms of the agreement are reasonable. The court should not assume that either is likely to commit his company to an agreement which he thinks is unfair, or which he thinks includes unreasonable terms. Unless satisfied that one party has, in effect, taken unfair advantage of the other – or that a term is so unreasonable that it cannot properly have been understood or considered – the court should not interfere.[1]

In almost all circumstances, when someone enters into a contract (whether through a licence agreement or a set of terms and conditions), their use of a product or service will be governed entirely by the contractual terms and not by copyright law. In short, where access to or use of content is governed by a set of terms and conditions or a licence agreement, the appropriate area of law is that of contract law rather than copyright law.

There are, however, two places in UK law where copyright law cannot be overridden by contract law. They relate to: the making of a backup copy of a computer program, and a lawful user of a database who extracts or re-utilizes insubstantial parts of the contents of the database.

1 Regarding back-up copies, CDPA 1998 Section 50 states:

(1) It is not an infringement of copyright for a lawful user of a copy of a computer program to make any back up copy of it which it is necessary for him to have for the purposes of his lawful use.

(2) For the purposes of this section and sections 50B and 50C a person is a lawful user of a computer program if (whether under a licence to do any acts restricted by the copyright in the program or otherwise), he has a right to use the program.

(3) Where an act is permitted under this section, it is irrelevant whether or not there exists any term or condition in an agreement which purports to prohibit or restrict the act (such terms being, by virtue of section 296A, void).

This section was inserted into the CDPA as a result of The Copyright (Computer Programs) Regulations 1992, SI 1922/3233.

2   Regarding what a lawful user of a database can do, the Copyright and Rights in Databases Regulations 1997 state:

Avoidance of certain terms affecting lawful users
Regulation 19. – (1) A lawful user of a database which has been made available to the public in any manner shall be entitled to extract or re-utilize insubstantial parts of the contents of the database for any purpose.
(2) Where under an agreement a person has a right to use a database, or part of a database, which has been made available to the public in any manner, any term or condition in the agreement shall be void in so far as it purports to prevent that person from extracting or re-utilizing insubstantial parts of the contents of the database, or of that part of the database, for any purpose.

6.3 Model licence agreements

Model licences are useful to draw upon for a number of reasons:

- The process of negotiating licences can be extremely time-consuming.
- If you have a lot of electronic products, you will potentially have a problem remembering the terms and conditions for each one,

which will create practical difficulties when trying to ensure that each agreement is being complied with.

- Model licences can be used to ensure that you have a basic set of rights.
- They can provide a useful starting point for contract negotiations.
- They contain the form of words necessary to express most of the variables that publishers and librarians are likely to meet when negotiating licence terms.

It is well worth looking at the range of model licences available to see whether any that fit well with your type of organization.

There have been a number of initiatives to produce model licence agreements, such as the ones from ECUP, JISC and John Cox Associates. There are standard agreements available for a range of different institutional types such as public libraries national libraries, university libraries and company libraries – see Table 6.1.

Table 6.1 Standard agreements available

	Companies	Universities	Public libraries	National libraries
European Copyright User Platform (ECUP)	Heads of agreement	Heads of agreement	Heads of agreement	Heads of agreement
Joint Information Systems Committee (JISC) (www.jisc.ac.uk)		Model e-journal licence		
John Cox Associates (www.johncoxassociates.com)	Licence and Commentary	Single academic institutions Commentary Academic consortia Commentary	Licence and Commentary	
NESLI (www.nesli2.ac.uk)		Model NESLI site licence		

Further information

American Library Association et al., *Principles for Licensing Electronic Resources*, www.arl.com/sc/licensing/licprinciples.shtml.

Association of Research Libraries, *Let There be Light: proceedings summary*, http://arl.org.

Copyright Management for Scholarship, *Zwolle Principles* and also *Copyright Toolkit for Author/Publisher Agreements*, www.surf.nl/copyright/keyissues/scholarlycommunication/agreements.php.

International Coalition of Library Consortia (1998) *Statement of Current Perspectives and Preferred Practices for the Selection and Purchase of Electronic Information*, www.library.yale.edu/consortia/statement.html. See also two updates: *Update No. 1: new developments in e-journal licensing* (2001), and *Update No. 2, Pricing and Economics* (2004).

International Federation of Library Associations and Institutions, IFLA Committee on Copyright and Other Legal Matters (2001) *Licensing Principles*, www.ifla.org/v/ebpb/copy.htm.

National Humanities Alliance (2002) *Basic Principles for Managing Intellectual Property in the Digital Environment*, www.nhalliance.org/ip/ip_principles.html.

Technical Advisory Service for Images, *Example Licence Agreement*, www.tasi.ac.uk/advice/managing/licence1.html.

Tilburg University, *Library Licensing Principles*, http://webdoc.sub.gwdg.de/ebook/aw/prinzliz/1_lizp-e.htm.

6.4 Licences from the CLA and NLA

It is important to recognize that collective licensing societies such as the Copyright Licensing Agency (CLA) and the Newspaper Licensing Agency (NLA) are in effect only the middle-men. They represent the interests of rightsholders. The CLA, for example, works on behalf of the ALCS and PLS, who represent authors and publishers respectively, and also works closely with DACS, who represent visual artists.

Collecting societies can only act where they have been given a mandate and, so far, rightsholders have been reluctant to let the collecting societies administer their rights in 'born digital' content. The rightsholders often don't want anything to compete directly with the primary sales of their digital publications.

One thing to watch out for is that the range of material covered by a digitization licence is likely to be smaller than that covered by a hard copy licence. In the case of the NLA, for example, none of the News International titles (*The Times*, *Sunday Times*, *News of the World* and *The*

Sun) are covered by the electronic licence,[2] while in the case of the CLA, licences do not at the time of writing cover digitizing anything from outside the UK.

6.4.1 Copyright Licensing Agency

The CLA provides licences on a sectoral basis. This section looks briefly at the licences for three sectors: further and higher education, general business and pharmaceutical. Details of the CLA licences available for each sector and their terms and conditions can be found at www.cla.co.uk/licensing/index.php.

In addition to the licences which are currently in place, the CLA has for some time been working on a project to create a comprehensive digital licence.

Trial scanning licence in further education

The FE sector has had a trial scanning licence in place since August 2003 (www.cla.co.uk/support/fe/index.html). In addition to all previous photocopying rights, the licence grants a number of scanning rights. Licensees can do any of the following subject to the detailed terms and conditions of the licence:

- scan extracts from books, journals and periodicals (UK licensed material)
- retype extracts from UK licensed material onto a computer
- store copies on individual PCs or a secure network
- incorporate digital copies into presentation software (such as MS PowerPoint)
- send copies by fax
- e-mail copies to authorized users
- use copies on a virtual learning environment (VLE), managed learning environment (MLE) or college intranet
- receive digital copies supplied under other CLA licences.

The FE scanning licence does not permit digital copies to be edited or manipulated or modified in any way. Staff are, however, allowed to mark copies (such as by highlighting or underlining) in order to add emphasis to a copied extract. Retyped extracts must be reproduced verbatim, including all punctuation. The use of optical character recognition (OCR) software is not permitted under the licence. Copies may not be placed on, or linked to, the internet except as part of a secure network.

The copying extent limitations (5%, one chapter, etc.) apply both to paper and digital copies. Photographs, illustrations, diagrams, etc. in licensed material are covered by the licence, both for paper and digital copies. However, stills, advertisements, logos and trademarks are not covered. Neither does the licence permit the production of slides, as there is a separate licence available from DACS for this purpose.

The trial licence authorizes the use of copies on MLEs, VLEs, college intranets or similar digital networks, so long as they comply with the licence definition of a secure network. The definition covers secure, password-protected access to a digital network irrespective of the location of the user logging in.

The licence does not cover e-learning resources. Anything originating in a digital format, for example e-books, online journals and other digital learning resources, is not covered by the licence and will usually be available on its own licensing terms.

It is a requirement of the licence that all extracts to be digitized include, where reasonably practicable, bibliographic details of the source such as author/artist, title, publisher and ISBN/ISSN.

Higher education trial licence for photocopying and scanning

The higher education trial licence for photocopying and scanning enables HE institutions (HEIs) to make multiple photocopies of limited extracts from most copyright protected printed books, journals and magazines, and also to make digital copies of limited extracts from most copyright protected printed books, journals and magazines for distribution or delivery to students enrolled on a course of study.

There are some important limitations that should be noted:

- Only material published in the UK may be scanned (as long as it does not appear on the list of 'Works Excluded from Scanning under the HE Trial Licence').
- Content cannot be copied if it is listed in the standard 'List of Excluded Categories and Excluded Works'.
- The licence does not authorize copying from born digital content: this would normally be governed by a set of terms and conditions or a licence agreement from the publisher.

For each digital copy prepared and distributed, the HEI is required: to append a copyright notice, and to record and report bibliographic and course-based details to the CLA.

The licensee is required to nominate a co-ordinator to supervise compliance with its terms, and the licence co-ordinator is responsible for:

- appointing members of staff designated to prepare/distribute digital copies
- verifying that each digital copy prepared incorporates a copyright notice
- ensuring that each digital copy distributed is recorded on a record sheet
- sending the digital copy record sheet to the CLA bi-annually
- liaising with the CLA's Compliance Unit on the conduct of audits or photocopying surveys, if and when required
- liaising with the CLA's Customer Services Department on distance learning and NCB (non-credit-bearing courses) returns.

When digital copies are made, they should be made from either an original of the book, journal or magazine owned by the HEI, or from a copyright fee-paid copy of a chapter/article supplied by an organization holding a document delivery licence with the CLA.

The extent limits – that is, how much can be photocopied – under the licence are:

- up to 5% or one chapter of a book
- up to 5% or one article of a journal issue

- up to 5% or one paper of one set of conference proceedings
- up to 5% or one report of a single case from a report of judicial proceedings
- up to 5% of an anthology of short stories or poems or one short story or one poem of not more than ten pages.

Digital copies can only be distributed via course-based collections, which could take place via a virtual learning environment or an intranet. However, HEIs are required to apply strict procedures for secure authentication (by some combination of user name, password and/or course enrolment key) to make sure that access to course collections is limited to authorized persons.

Provided that digital copies are organized in course collections, the licence permits any authorized person to view digital copies made for any course (which might apply when a student is deciding whether to enrol on a particular course). However, downloading or printing a digital copy is limited to the enrolled students plus the course tutor(s).

The licence agreement does not permit digital copies to be stored in 'open' resources, such as an institutional or subject repository, an electronic reserve or digital library, where delivery across course boundaries is enabled. But it does allow an extract of a book, journal or magazine to be made simultaneously available to students on more than one discrete course of study, or a digital copy of a different part of the same book, journal or magazine to be made available to students on another course of study.

Licensees are not obliged to make digital copies available for viewing by individuals other than those who are defined as course users.

The licence allows a student on a course of study (and the course tutor) to view, download and print a digital copy, but the rights granted do not extend to redistributing, reformatting or republishing the digital copy (or any part of it).

Business licence

The CLA introduced scanning and e-mail distribution to the standard business licence with effect from 1 October 2002.

With a CLA business licence, companies are able to scan, and distribute by e-mail, extracts from UK books, journals and magazines. Distribution of copyright extracts is also permitted from copies received from licensed third party digital material suppliers (such as the British Library).

Pharmaceutical licence

In May 2004, the CLA and the Association of the British Pharmaceutical Industry (ABPI) launched a digitization licence for pharmaceutical companies.

The licence permits scanning and e-mail delivery, in addition to photocopying, of articles from books, magazines and journals.

Under the CLA pharmaceutical licence, systematic electronic storage is permitted. This enables licensees to store electronic copies of certain materials on an intranet server for staff to access. Additionally, international distribution to affiliate companies is allowed (as long as these have been listed in Schedule 1 of the licence agreement), as is supplying copies to pharmaceutical regulatory authorities when seeking marketing authorization.

6.4.2 Newspaper Licensing Agency

The NLA provides an option for digital copying: when an organization applies for a NLA licence, there is an option on the licence application form to cover digital copying. Applicants for NLA licences have to indicate if they wish to copy digitally and/or distribute cuttings to their personnel and, if so, whether they intend to scan original cuttings internally, or whether instead they are intending to use a press cuttings agency/PR consultancy to deliver digital cuttings. They are also required to attach an audit of digital copying with their completed application form.

The digital licence does not cover born digital content, but rather the digitization by the licensee of newspaper cuttings from hard-copy newspapers. These can then be loaded onto an intranet or distributed by e-mail to multiple recipients. It doesn't, for example, cover the content of newspapers found on websites.

However, the licence agreement makes clear that NLA newspapers' cuttings must be permanently deleted from digital systems within seven days of scanning.

eClips

The NLA's eClips service is an electronic database of press cuttings, which delivers digital clippings to users via their press cuttings agencies. The database takes newspaper content directly from production systems. Images are processed and indexed using XML technology on a central host system in order to allow for rapid retrieval. The service includes a 'MyArchive' feature, which enables users to retain access to digital cuttings for a full year.

Further information

eClips blog, http://eclips.squarespace.com/blog.
NLA website, www.nla.co.uk.

6.5 Creative Commons

Creative Commons (http://creativecommons.org) was set up by copyright lawyers in the United States – Lawrence Lessing was the founder and is the chairman. Creative Commons aims to provide alternative licences which can be attached to creative content. Indeed, the legally binding Creative Commons licences define the spectrum of possibilities between full copyright (all rights reserved) and the public domain (no rights reserved), with a range of licence types available. Creative Commons licences can, for example, include:

- a demand that the content be used only for non-commercial work
- a demand that any content the work is used to create be given the same Creative Commons licence
- permission for content to be given freely to the public domain with no rights attached whatsoever.

Creative Commons licences help content producers retain copyright while at the same time encouraging certain uses of their work. This is best expressed in the phrase 'some rights reserved'.

The initial licence agreements were based on the US legal model, but Creative Commons UK was launched in the second half of 2004 (http://creativecommons.org/worldwide/uk).

Searching for Creative Commons content

http://search.creativecommons.org/
http://search.yahoo.com/cc
http://www.commoncontent.org
Google Advanced Search (see the 'Usage Rights' drop-down menu)

There is a catalogue of web content which uses Creative Commons licences available at www.commoncontent.org.

Creative Commons licences use symbols to indicate at a glance what can and what cannot be done with a work. These include symbols for:

- Attribution: you let others copy, distribute, display and perform your copyrighted work – and derivative works based on it – but only if they give credit in the way you request.
- Non-commercial: you let others copy, distribute, display and perform your work – and derivative works based on it – but for non-commercial purposes only.
- No derivative works: you let others copy, distribute, display and perform only verbatim copies of your work, and not derivative works based on it.
- ShareAlike: you allow others to distribute derivative works only under a licence identical to the licence that governs your work (note: a licence cannot feature both the ShareAlike and no derivative works options – the ShareAlike requirement applies only to derivative works).

6.6 Open access

Open access is an alternative to the traditional method of publishing scholarly papers. In the open access system, electronic versions of scholarly materials are made available free of charge to anyone who wishes to read them. A directory of open access journals can be found at www.doaj.org.

There are two ways in which open access is achieved. Articles can be:

- published in open access journals which don't levy a subscription charge to the user
- deposited in an institution's electronic repository which is accessible from remote locations without any access restrictions.

Just as in the traditional publishing market, some open access journals are peer-reviewed, whereby papers are submitted, reviewed, authenticated and finally published. Open access journals are subject to thorough quality controls; many open access journals are supported by editors who organize the refereeing process.

One of the drivers for the adoption of open access is the so-called serials crisis. Academic institutions aren't able to stock all of the journal titles relevant to their research staff for a number of reasons which, when considered together, amount to the serials crisis:

- the large number of journals published
- journal prices increasing at a much faster than inflation
- constraints on library budgets.

Financial considerations are, however, not the only driver for the adoption of open access. In fact, one of the main motives is to grant academic peers and scientific collaborators rapid access to discoveries in a field of study by publishing on the internet.

There are a number of different models for open access, including one which is known as 'author-pays'. Under the author-pays model, the author has to pay a fee in order to have an article published. Although the author has to pay for the article to be published, under this model the user doesn't have to pay anything to access the item. It is made available to users free of charge.

The general principles of open access require authors to grant an irrevocable right for anybody to download, copy, redistribute and view the content that is submitted. Copyright still subsists within the published material, and there are a number of important considerations that need to be borne in mind:

- Any copying and redistribution of the content should always include the proper attribution.
- The author's moral right of integrity does not permit modification of a work.

The copyright policy would not normally permit printing of copies in large numbers, especially if this was for commercial use, although a suitable number of private printouts is generally permitted. The SHERPA website has drawn together links to various publishers' copyright policies and self archiving: see www.sherpa.ac.uk/romeo.php?all=yes.

In October 2003 the Berlin Declaration on Open Access to Knowledge in the Sciences and Humanities was signed by the Max Planck Society and a number of other large German and international research organizations. Signatories to the Berlin Declaration agreed to make progress by:

- encouraging their researchers or grant recipients to publish their work according to the principles of open access
- encouraging cultural institutions to support open access by providing their resources on the internet
- developing means and ways to evaluate open access contributions in order to maintain the standards of quality assurance and good scientific practice, and advocating that such publications be recognized in promotion and tenure evaluation.

There are a number of declarations similar to the Berlin Declaration, such as the Bethesda Declaration of Open Access Publishing and the Budapest Open Access Initiative.

Further information

Bebbington, Laurence (2001) *Managing Content: licensing, copyright and privacy issues in managing electronic resources*, www.biall.org.uk/docs/pulimvin2bebb.pdf.

Bielefield, Arlene and Cheeseman, Lawrence (1999) *Interpreting and Negotiating Licensing Agreements*, Neal-Schuman.

Giavarra, Emanuella (2001) *Licensing Digital Resources: how to avoid the legal pitfalls*, 2nd edn, EBLIDA (European Bureau of Library, Information and Documentation Associations).

House of Commons. Science and Technology Committee (2004) *Scientific Publications: free for all?* HC 399, 2004, www.publications.parliament.uk/pa/cm200304/cmselect/cmsctech/399/399 02.htm.

Nielsen, Henning P. and Whittall, Jane (2000) Model Licensing: key elements and specific needs in electronic journal licensing for the pharmaceutical industry, *Serials*, **13** (2), 103–9, www.p-d-r.com/publications/nielsen.pdf.

Publishers Association (1999) *Copyright Licensing in an Electronic Environment*, www.publishers.org.uk/paweb/paweb.nsf/homepages/guidelines+(public)! opendocument.

SHERPA, www.sherpa.ac.uk.

World Intellectual Property Organization (2003) *World Intellectual Property on the Internet: a survey of the issues*, www.wipo.org/copyright/ecommerce/en/html.

Notes

1 Watford Electronics v Sanderson 2001 EWCA Civ 317 para 55.
2 The News International titles are, however, available through the eClips service (see page 95).

7

Educational establishments

7.1 Introduction

The higher and further education sector needs to be able to put together materials in digital form which can then be loaded onto a virtual or managed learning environment (VLE or MLE). The goal is to provide seamless access to all electronic materials. The benefits of doing this are:

- A VLE makes material accessible: indeed, a number of users can simultaneously access the same course materials.
- Items such as journal articles don't go missing or get damaged if they are part of a digital library.
- Access to the system is controlled, and it is therefore secure.
- Distance learning students who have remote access to the VLE have access to a wider range of resources than would otherwise be the case.

Copyright law is the main barrier standing in the way of putting together a resource of this kind. It is important to ensure that the necessary rights and permissions are obtained. Dealing with publishers, negotiating licence agreements and/or obtaining copyright clearance can be something of a daunting task. It can also be extremely time-consuming. There is the whole process of trying to identify the copyright holder, tracking him/her down and asking for copyright clearance, and often the rightsholders have to be chased up before copyright clearance is finally agreed.

In an article by Koulouris and Kapidakis (2005), the access and reproduction policies of the digital collections of ten university digital libraries worldwide are examined. They show how acquisition methods and copyright ownership affect the access and reproduction policies of digital collections.

It is worth mentioning that Recommendation 2 of the Gowers Review addresses the need for copyright law to reflect the way in which teaching is now undertaken: 'Enable educational provisions to cover distance learning and interactive whiteboards by 2008 by amending sections 35 and 36 of the CDPA 1988.' This recommendation will be implemented in due course.

Some copyright staff at universities and colleges will organize copyright clearance for extracts from books and journal articles, and also for hyperlinks when these are deep links. They might also organize the digitization of content, and facilitate remote access for distance learners to copyright-cleared material.

Many in the educational sector use the HERON service, a division of Ingenta, rather than trying to sort out the copyright clearance in-house. HERON offers the only national service to the UK academic community for copyright clearance, digitization and delivery of book extracts and journal articles. It has also developed a resource bank of digitized materials for rapid re-use (subject to copyright permissions). See www.heron.ingenta.com/.

When course tutors put together a list of core reading materials, they may well do so without taking into account the cost involved. If, however, they are made aware during the course development stage of the varying costs charged for copyright-cleared articles by different publishers, this could well influence their choice of recommended reading.

Otherwise, it may be that the following year some of the content from the more expensive publishers is substituted by articles which are available at a cheaper rate or even free of charge.

It is worth investigating, for example, whether the publisher has a policy of allowing educational establishments to make use of journal articles free of charge if they subscribe to the titles either in hard copy or electronic formats.

The collection of materials that is assembled for a course may consist of a mixture of free and chargeable items, hyperlinks and also items written by the course tutor.

7.1.1 Definition of educational establishments

The Copyright (Educational Establishments) Order 2005: SI 2005/223, made under Section 174(1)(b) of the CDPA 1988, lists those educational establishments that may take advantage of certain copyright exceptions for the purposes of:

- making multiple copies for visually impaired persons
- performing, playing or showing work in the course of their activities
- recording of broadcasts
- reprographic copying of passages from published works
- lending of copies.

7.2 Educational Recording Agency

The Copyright (Certification of Licensing Scheme for Educational Recording of Broadcasts) (Educational Recording Agency Limited) Order 2007: SI 2007/266 certifies the licensing scheme operated by the Educational Recording Agency Limited for the granting of licences to educational establishments for the recording by them of broadcasts, other than television programmes broadcast on behalf of the Open University.

Each ERA recording should be marked with the name of the broadcaster, the date upon which the broadcast took place and the title of that recording. Indeed, in order to meet the licence requirements, all copies must be marked with a statement in clear and bold lettering reading: 'This recording is to be used only for non-commercial educational purposes under the terms of the ERA licence.'

7.2.1 Rights bestowed by the ERA Licence

(a) to cause or authorise the making of recordings of a broadcast and copies of such a recording and (only as a direct result of their inclusion in a broadcast) of copyright works and/or performances contained in the recorded broadcast by or on behalf of an Educational Establishment for the educational purposes of that Educational Establishment ("ERA Recordings"); and

(b) to authorise ERA Recordings to be communicated to the public by a person situated within the premises of an Educational Establishment but only to the extent that the communication cannot be received by any person situated outside the premises of that Educational Establishment.

No recording or copying of a broadcast under any Licence shall be made except by or on behalf of an Educational Establishment and any such recording or copying shall be made either:

a) on the premises of the Educational Establishment by or under the direct supervision of a teacher or employee of the Licensee; or

b) at the residence of a teacher employed by the Licensee by that teacher; or

c) at the premises of a third party authorised by the Licensee to make recordings or copies on behalf of the Licensee under written contractual terms and conditions which prevent the retention or use of any recordings or copies by that third party or any other third party unless ERA shall have expressly agreed that a specific third party may retain any recordings or copies for subsequent use only by authorised Licensees of ERA in accordance with the provisions of the Licensing Scheme.

To provide sufficient acknowledgement all copies shall be marked with a statement in clear and bold lettering:

'This recording is to be used only for non-commercial educational purposes under the terms of the ERA Licence' or such other wording or statement as ERA shall reasonably require from time to time.

Physical copies shall include the statement on the exterior of the copy, and/or its packaging.

When under the Licence copies are made and stored in digital form for access through a computer server, the statement shall also be included as a written opening credit or webpage which must be viewed or listened to before access to the ERA Recording is permitted.

Licensees shall undertake that if and when any ERA Recordings are communicated to the public by a person situated within the premises of an Educational Establishment under the Licence, suitable password and other digital rights management or technological protection systems are operated and applied by the Licensee to ensure that such communication is not received or receivable by persons situated outside the premises of the licensed Educational Establishment.

Licensees shall be required to take all reasonable steps to ensure that rights granted by a Licence are not exceeded or abused by teachers, employees, pupils or other persons.

7.3 Open University

Programmes broadcast by the Open University are the subject of a separate licensing scheme in the UK operated by the Open University Worldwide Limited – The Copyright (Certification of Licensing Scheme for Educational Recordings of Broadcasts) (Open University) Order 2003: SI 2003/187.

Where no licence is available and there is no contractual restriction, then the broadcast may be copied anyway. This is useful for copying overseas broadcasts, for example.

7.4 Electronic reserves

The practice of making recommended reading materials available electronically as 'e-reserves' is growing among academic institutions.

In the USA, there has been a dispute between the University of California, San Diego's library and the American Association of Publishers on this matter (Graham, 2005). The AAP is concerned that e-reserves can infringe their copyright and have an adverse effect on sales. If a compromise solution cannot be found, this could lead to the possibility of legal action.

Since e-reserves are behind the firewalls of academic institutions, there is no transparency in terms of just how extensive the recommended reading materials actually are. However, in the UK there is always the possibility that publishers might make a request to find out under the Freedom of Information Act 2000, since the HE and FE sectors are both subject to its provisions.

7.5 Electronic theses

In the first quarter of 2007, a two-year project – EThOSnet – was launched (see www.ethos.ac.uk). The intention is to establish a live service in 2009 run by the British Library to take us a step nearer to a fully integrated national electronic theses service.

JISC and CURL (the Consortium of Research Libraries), with the support of participating libraries, are funding the EThOSnet project to widen access to a rich and vast but until now largely untapped resource for researchers. The intention is for the EThOS service to make UK theses openly available for global use, providing an international showcase for some of the best of UK research. It is also anticipated that EThOS will become a core element of the UK's national research infrastructure.

The project builds on earlier exploratory work, also funded by JISC and CURL, which between 2004 and 2006 developed a prototype for the service. Independent evaluation has since given the prototype strong backing and suggested further developments.

Further information

Aberystwyth Learning and Teaching Online (2003) *Copyright and Virtual Learning Environments*, University of Wales, Aberystwyth, http://alto.aber.ac.uk/Bb/helpsheets/copyright.pdf.

Andrew, Theo (2004) *Intellectual Property and Electronic Theses*, JISC,
www.jisclegal.ac.uk/pdfs/ethesepaper.doc.

Casey, John (2004) *Intellectual Property Rights in Networked e-Learning*,
www.jisclegal.ac.uk/pdfs/johncasey_word_version.rtf.

Graham, Marty (2005) Sides Clash over Online Library, *The National Law
Journal*, (29 April), www.law.com/jsp/article.jsp?id=1114679112558.

JISC Legal (2005) *Copyright and e-Learning in FE: interview with Alan Rae,
Copyright Advisor to the Association of Scottish Colleges* (video),
www.jisclegal.ac.uk/publications/Copyright_Video_AR/Content.htm.

JISC Legal (2007) *Copyright and e-Learning Workshop* (PowerPoint slides),
www.jisclegal.ac.uk/events/RSCCopyright05.htm.

JISC Legal (2007) *Investigation into Student Work and IPR*,
www.jisclegal.ac.uk/publications/studentipr.htm.

Koulouris, Alexandros and Kapidakis, Sarantos (2005) Access and
Reproduction Policies of University Digital Collections, *Journal of
Librarianship and Information Science*, **37** (1), 25–33.

Secker, Jane (2004) *Electronic Resources in the Virtual Learning Environment:
a practical guide for librarians*, Chandos Publishing.

8

Authors' rights

8.1 Introduction

The author as first owner of copyright has a number of economic and moral rights. Moral rights are concerned with the protection of the personality and reputation of an author.

Moral rights cannot be assigned to anyone else, but they can be waived by authors if they do so in writing. Furthermore, moral rights are not infringed by any act to which the person entitled to the right has consented.

On the other hand, authors can assign their economic rights. For example, they might assign some or all of these economic rights to a publisher.

8.2 Economic rights

The economic rights are exclusive rights of the author. They are set out in Section 16 of the CDPA as amended:

16. – (1) The owner of the copyright in a work has, in accordance with the following provisions of this Chapter, the exclusive right to do the following acts in the United Kingdom –

(a) to copy the work (see section 17);

(b) to issue copies of the work to the public (see section 18);

(ba) to rent or lend the work to the public (see section 18A);

(c) to perform, show or play the work in public (see section 19);

(d) to communicate the work to the public (see section 20);

(e) to make an adaptation of the work or do any of the above in relation to an adaptation (see section 21)...

8.2.1 Right of communication to the public

The Copyright and Related Rights Regulations 2003 introduced a new right for copyright owners relating to the communication of a work to the public, specifically where this is done by electronic means. This exclusive right is set out in Section 20 of the CDPA 1988, which says:

Section 20: Infringement by communication to the public

(1) The communication to the public of the work is an act restricted by the copyright in –

(a) a literary, dramatic, musical or artistic work,

(b) a sound recording or film, or

(c) a broadcast.

(2) References in this Part to communication to the public are to communication to the public by electronic transmission, and in relation to a work include –

(a) the broadcasting of the work;

(b) the making available to the public of the work by electronic transmission in such a way that members of the public may access it from a place and at a time individually chosen by them.

The right of communication to the public would certainly cover putting material onto a website. This is significant – it means that if anyone wishes to include someone else's work on a website it is absolutely essential that they first obtain permission.

In addition to the right of communication to the public, there is also a similar right for performers, which is introduced by the Copyright and Related Rights Regulations, called the making the work available right. This new right enables performers to control the use of recordings of their performances in the same way that a copyright owner can control communication of the work to the public. The right is defined as the right to prevent anyone making available to the public a recording of a performance by electronic transmission so that members of the public may access the recording from a place and at a time chosen by them. In other words, performers can control the use of recordings of their performances on a website. This is important if one wants to use, say, a video clip as part of one's website presentation.

➡ Relevant legal cases

Sociedad General de Autores y Editores de España v Rafael Hoteles SA (Case C-306/05)

In answering questions referred to it by a Spanish court, the European Court of Justice confirmed that the transmission by hotel owners of broadcasts through television sets in hotel rooms is a 'communication to the public', and could therefore constitute an infringement of copyright under Article 3(1) of the Copyright Directive (2001/29 EC). The court held that the private nature of hotel rooms did not preclude the communication of works in these rooms from being a 'communication to the public', since the test was whether a communication had been made to 'the public', not whether a communication occurred in a public or private place.

8.3 Moral rights

In the UK, people tend to emphasize the economic rights of the author as first owner of copyright over and above moral rights. But the authors of literary, dramatic, musical and artistic works, and also film directors, have a series of moral rights conferred on them by the Copyright Act 1988:

- the right of **paternity** (ss.77–79)
- the right of **integrity** (s.80)
- the right to **object to false attribution** (s.84)
- the right of **disclosure** (s.85)

8.3.1 The right of paternity

This is the right of the author to be identified as such wherever a work is published, performed or broadcast. It is also known as the right of attribution.

Article 5 of the Berne Copyright Convention for the Protection of Literary and Artistic Works 1886 says that these rights 'shall not be subject to any formality'. A number of copyright experts argue that the UK's implementation of an author's moral rights in the CDPA 1988 does not comply with the Berne Copyright Convention's requirement that there should be no formalities before authors are afforded their rights. In UK law, the right of paternity cannot be infringed unless it has been asserted. Such a requirement would seem to constitute a formality. It is because of this requirement for an author to assert the right that a statement will normally be found at the front of books saying something along the lines of 'Joe Bloggs asserts his right under the Copyright, Designs and Patents Act 1988 to be identified as the author of this work.'

A publisher's contract might say:

The Author asserts his moral right to be identified as the Author of the work in relation to all such rights as are granted by the Author to the Publisher under the terms and conditions of this Agreement.

The Publisher hereby undertakes:
– to print on the verso title page of every copy of every edition of the work published by him in the United Kingdom the words 'The right of [Joe Bloggs] to be identified as the author of this work has been asserted by him in accordance with the Copyright, Designs and Patents Act 1988.'

There are a number of exceptions to this right. It does not apply, for example:

- to computer programs
- to designs of typefaces
- to computer-generated works
- where the material is used in magazines and newspapers or reference works such as encyclopaedias or dictionaries
- to works generated in the course of employment.

The paternity right is strengthened in the Copyright and Related Rights Regulations 2003, in the sense that it is now an offence to tamper with or remove electronic rights management information. If there is a copyright notice on an electronic work, and this clearly identifies the author, it would be an offence to remove that notice.

8.3.2 The right of integrity

Section 80 of the CDPA 1988 sets out the right of an author to prevent or object to derogatory treatment of his/her work (also known as the right of integrity). This right is granted to the authors of literary, dramatic, musical and artistic works, and also to film directors.

Treatment of a work would be considered derogatory if it amounts to distortion or mutilation of the work or is otherwise prejudicial to the honour or reputation of the author or director. If authors wish to object to derogatory treatment, they need to demonstrate that their work has been subject to some sort of alteration, which might include additions to the work, removal of parts of the work or adaptation.

Section 81 of the CDPA 1988 sets out a number of exceptions to the right of integrity. It does not apply to translation or transposition of the key or register of a musical work, to computer programs or computer-generated works, to any work made for the purposes of reporting current events or to publication in newspapers, periodicals, encyclopaedias or similar works.

The right of integrity is automatic, without any formalities. It subsists for as long as the work in question remains in copyright. It applies to copies published commercially, copies of a sound recording or film made available to the public, performance, public display and broadcasting.

Rights are granted to broadcasters to alter works where, for example, laws of public decency might be contravened or good taste might be offended, or works which might be seen to be incitements to crime, violence or terrorism.

Right of integrity and digital works

Digitization can have a significant impact on a work. It has the potential to allow complete fragmentation, reassembly and redistribution of all or part of a work. When an author assents to the digitization of a work, then they should consider whether or not to specify that any digital copy must appear in an unaltered form, or whether they will permit any kind of alteration.

The Copyright Licensing Agency recognizes that the manipulation of images or text is a moral issue, and as such is outside their remit. The CLA's licences are carefully designed to protect the interests of the rightsholders they represent. Frequently these are moral rights, and the licences are very clear on issues such as manipulation of text or images. When an artist asks, 'But wouldn't the end-user crop or stretch my image?', or an author asks, 'Couldn't my text be tampered with?', the answer is: 'No. Not under a CLA licence.'

8.3.3 The right to object to false attribution

This is the right of the authors of literary, dramatic, musical and artistic works and film directors not to have a work or film falsely attributed to them. The right lasts for 20 years after the death of the person to whom a work has been falsely attributed.

8.3.4 The right of disclosure

This is the right to privacy of a person who commissions the taking of a photograph or the making of a film for private and domestic purposes. Under the CDPA 1988 this would apply to a person who commissions a photograph or film but then decides not to have it issued to the public, exhibited or shown in public, or included in a broadcast.

8.3.5 Duration and ownership of moral rights

The rights of paternity and integrity last as long as the copyright in the work; they do not apply when work is published in a newspaper, magazine or similar periodical, or to contributions to an encyclopaedia, dictionary, yearbook or other collective work of reference.

When an author dies, the rights pass to whoever is nominated in the author's will. If no direction is given in a will, the rights pass to the person receiving the copyright. However, the right of a person not to have a work falsely attributed to him/her is only actionable by an author's personal representatives.

Further information

Frankel, Mark (2002) *Seizing the Moment: scientists' authorship rights in the digital age*, American Association for the Advancement of Science, www.aaas.org/spp/sfrl/projects/epub/finalreport.pdf.

Salokannel, Marjut and Strowel, Alain (2000) *Study Contract Concerning Moral Rights in the Context of the Exploitation of Works through Digital Technology*, European Commission, Internal Market Directorate General.

9

Other issues

9.1 The international dimension

In the digital world, international issues are both highly relevant and particularly important. Copyright doesn't somehow cease to be an issue when one reaches the borders of a country:

- If one were to place content on a publicly available website, this could potentially be accessed throughout the world.
- If one posted the back issues of an electronic journal that had been received in PDF format onto a global intranet, this could also be problematic unless one had used passwords in order to restrict

access to that item to those for whom the necessary permissions had been obtained.

- If an employee receives an electronic copy of a report by e-mail, it would be easy for them to forward that item on to huge numbers of people all over the world within a matter of seconds, but if an e-mail is opened by someone based outside the UK, then that copy is subject to the copyright law of the country in which it is received.

The Berne Convention for the Protection of Literary and Artistic Works is the most important agreement covering international copyright. The Convention is administered by the WIPO and signatories to the convention are required to ensure that reciprocal treatment is given to a copyrighted work in virtually every country (a listing of the signatories to the convention can be found at www.wipo.int/treaties/en/ShowResults.jsp?lang=en&treaty_id=15).

When copyright infringement occurs, what is important so far as the Berne Convention is concerned is where the alleged infringement actually took place. However, it can be extremely difficult to track down precisely where an infringement took place, or where the instructions to make the infringing copy came from. With material that has been placed on the web, there is the problem of copyright 'havens' – certain countries have a rather lax attitude to upholding intellectual property rights.

The copyright laws of EU member states are quite strict, but there is a question mark over their ability to enforce effectively the rights they conferred upon the creators of works. In light of these issues, rightsholders have successfully lobbied at a European Union level for a directive on the enforcement of intellectual property rights (2004/48/EC). In addition, there is a forthcoming directive on criminal measures aimed at ensuring the enforcement of intellectual property rights (see COM (2005) 276 final).

A number of people look to reproduction rights organizations (RROs) to provide them with a 'one-stop shop' where they can take out a single licence to cover their activities. However, it is important to bear in mind that RROs merely act as go-betweens; to be in a position to provide such a comprehensive solution, they need to be given the necessary mandates by the rightsholders. Do those mandates, for example, only cover material that is

produced in hard copy, or do they also cover digital content? When RROs
are given the authority to act on rightsholders' behalf internationally, they
are then in a position to reach reciprocal agreements with other RROs. The
International Federation of Reproduction Rights Organizations (IFRRO;
see www.ifrro.org) exists to provide a forum for co-operation between RROs.

The UK's Copyright Licensing Agency has a standard business licence
which permits scanning. However, while the licence covers a number of
countries other than the UK,[1] this is only true for hard copy content. The
business licence does not currently cover the digitization of content published outside the UK.

Even though there are a number of international copyright treaties and
conventions, and even though the European Commission has endeavoured
to develop a harmonized approach to intellectual property rights in order
to develop a single market whereby it is not more advantageous to do business with one country than another on the basis of its copyright laws, the
truth is that we do not have a situation where the copyright laws of each
country around the world have been completely harmonized. Instead, we
are in the rather unsatisfactory position that every situation needs to be
assessed on a country by country basis.

For example, an accountancy firm in country X wants to copy an article in an accountancy journal and circulate it by e-mail to accountants
internally, including those in overseas offices. Is there an RRO or collecting society in the countries where one wants to circulate the article? If
so, then these should be approached first and in most cases a licence fee
should be paid. The alternative is to approach the copyright owner directly in order to obtain their permission.

Some people have asked whether the CLA could provide a complete
indemnity to people in the UK copying foreign material, even if it comes
from countries that the CLA does not have reciprocal agreements with.
To achieve this the CLA would have to negotiate an insurance policy to
indemnify itself against any legal actions for copyright infringement; if
an insurance company willing to take on those risks could be found, the
fee for the policy would inevitably have to be passed on to licensees.

An author's work will be protected overseas automatically in the
same way that it is in the UK. This is because the UK is a member (i.e.

a signatory or contracting party) of several international conventions in this field:

- the Berne Convention for the Protection of Literary and Artistic Works (administered by the WIPO)
- the Rome Convention for the Protection of Performers, Producers of Phonograms and Broadcasting Organizations (administered by the WIPO)
- the Universal Copyright Convention (UCC), which is administered by the United Nations Educational, Scientific and Cultural Organization (UNESCO)
- the World Trade Organization agreement on Trade-Related Aspects of Intellectual Property Rights (TRIPS), whereby works are protected in WTO countries
- the WIPO Copyright Treaty.

Copyright material created by UK nationals or residents and falling within the scope of one of these conventions is automatically protected in each member country of the convention by the national law of that country. Most countries belong to at least the Berne Convention and/or the UCC.

The law on copyright and related rights in the CDPA 1988 extends to the whole of the UK, although it does not extend to the Channel Islands or to the Isle of Man.[2] However, material that does not have its origin in the UK is not necessarily automatically protected in the UK. In order to give effect to our obligations under various international conventions, treaties and other agreements, an Order in Council (in the form of a statutory instrument) has been made under Section 159 of the CDPA 1988 – The Copyright and Performances (Application to Other Countries) Order 2007: SI 2007/273 (see www.opsi.gov.uk/si/si2007/20070273.htm). This statutory instrument specifies the countries to which Part I of the CDPA 1988 applies.

9.2 Copyright compliance

Library and information professionals want advice and guidance on copyright law which is both clear and straightforward in order to ensure that they are complying with their legal obligations. However, it is not easy to come up with definitive guidance which will apply equally to all situations. There are several reasons for this.

One reason relates to the role of case law in the legal system of England and Wales. It is not enough simply to look at the relevant copyright legislation in the form of Acts of Parliament and Statutory Instruments. In this country, case law also has an important part to play: it creates precedents which are binding upon other courts which are at the same or a lower level in the hierarchy. To find out what the law says and means, it is therefore necessary both to look up the relevant legislation (and to ensure that what you are looking at is completely up to date and incorporates any annotations, where that is appropriate) and to seek out any relevant case law which can shed light on how the courts have interpreted that particular aspect of copyright law.

A second reason for there being so much legal uncertainty is that some of the most important words and phrases in the CDPA 1988 are not defined. They include:

- original
- substantial
- reasonable
- fair dealing
- copying for a commercial purpose.

Because there is so much legal uncertainty, copyright issues are really a question of working out how best to minimize the risk of being accused of copyright infringement.

If you want a brief statement on how to comply with digital copyright law, then it is best to consult the CILIP copyright posters (see www.cilip.org.uk/professionalguidance/copyright/formsandposters/posters.htm). There are, in fact, two CILIP copyright posters, and these are both relevant to digital content. The gold poster covers photocopying and scanning, while the blue poster covers downloading from websites and

Figure 9.1 CILIP copyright poster

databases (see Figure 9.1). Both posters provide guidance regarding what may be copied under the fair dealing exceptions which deal with research for a non-commercial purpose or private study.

Commentators have in the past spoken of there being three fair dealing exceptions. Now that the legislation distinguishes much more clearly between research and private study, I think it would be more accurate to think of there being four fair dealing exceptions:

- research
- private study
- criticism or review
- news reporting.

However, the posters only provide guidance relating to the fair dealing exceptions for research and private study. Key things to remember are:

- The research and private study exceptions only cover copying which is for *a non-commercial purpose*.
- If you are relying on the research and private study exceptions to justify your copying, these would only permit the downloading or printing of a single copy, and not the making of multiple copies (note that in the context of electronic information, placing a copy of a work onto an intranet, extranet, website or other shared drive would constitute the equivalent of multiple copying).
- *The source must be acknowledged,* unless it is impracticable to do so.

What can be digitized?

The following can be digitized:

- content which one has generated oneself
- content which is in the public domain
- a fair dealing copy for non-commercial research or private study of:
  — one chapter or 5%
  — one journal article
  — one short story or poem from an anthology
  (these are sometimes known as the 'safe copying limits').

But remember:

- only make a single copy
- don't put it onto a networked drive or shared resource.

- *Respect copyright notices on websites* and any copyright statements attached to works.
- Databases are normally governed by *contractual conditions*.

9.2.1 Copyright audit

Consider carrying out an audit of your current activities. For example, if you receive a number of journals in your library's e-mail inbox, and you have rules set up so your e-mail software automatically forwards these to the relevant people, particularly if these are sent to multiple recipients, you should ask:

- Do you have the necessary permissions to do this?
- Do you attach a covering note which reminds users of their obligations not to distribute the e-journal further?

The statement below is designed for use when supplying an electronic copy of a journal article:

> Please be aware that we have paid the copyright fee for only one copy of this article. If you need another copy, let me know and we will order another copy and pay the appropriate fees. Please delete the electronic copy of the article after you print a paper copy.

As part of a copyright audit, you need to think about electronic content. Questions to ask include:

- If you have a number of books which came with a CD-ROM, have you made a complete copy of the CD in case the original is lost?
- Have you copied back issues of e-journals onto a shared drive on the computer network?
- Have any works been posted onto your intranet in which you do not own the copyright?
- Do your users share their passwords to online services with friends and colleagues?

Remember

When copying works in electronic form:

■ Respect copyright notices on websites
■ Only download or print single copies unless specifically authorized to copy more.

When you have built up a complete picture of current practices and procedures, ask yourself whether you have permission for these activities. Authorization could come in a number of different ways:

• by the direct permission of the rightsholder
• by statute in the form of a copyright exception or permitted act
• through a set of terms and conditions or contract governing use of a product
• through a licence from an intermediary such as a collective licensing society acting on behalf of the rightsholder.

9.2.2 Ethics

Copyright compliance is both a legal issue and an ethical issue. In addition to the need to ensure that your activities remain on the right side of the law, there is also the need to ensure that your conduct as an information professional is ethical.

CILIP's ethical principles and code of professional practice (www.cilip.org.uk/professionalguidance/ethics) make it clear, for example, that the conduct of members should be characterized by 'respect for, and understanding of, the integrity of information items and for the intellectual effort of those who created them' and that CILIP members should 'defend the legitimate needs and interests of information users, while upholding the moral and legal rights of the creators and distributors of intellectual property'.

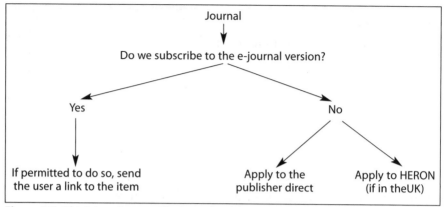

Figure 9.2 Obtaining clearance for journal articles

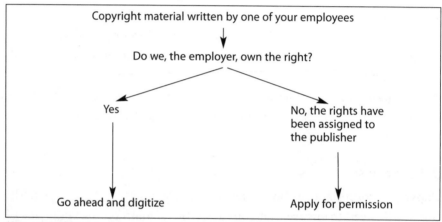

Figure 9.3 Obtaining clearance for own material

9.3 Copyright clearance

To clear copyright, you must gain permission from the copyright holder. Where it has not been possible to track down the rightsowner even after reasonable enquiry, the question that you have to ask is: What do we have to do to show that we've made all possible efforts to clear copyright? This will be clarified by the UK Intellectual Property Office once it implements Recommendation 14a of the Gowers Review: 'The Patent Office should issue clear guidance on the parameters of a "reasonable search" for orphan works, in consultation with rights holders, collecting societies, rights owners and archives, when an orphan works exception comes into being.'

You can take a number of steps to clear copyright (see, for example, Figures 9.2 and 9.3), but the most important thing to remember is to document all your efforts. Keep a 'due diligence' file which records all you do: all communications sent and any replies that you have received (both positive and negative). You are much less likely to be prosecuted if you can present evidence of your good intentions, and if a case is brought against you, the penalty will probably be minimal.

9.3.1 Steps in the copyright clearance process

1 Identify and locate the copyright owner. Use tools such as telephone directories and directories of artists/authors. If the owner is anonymous, then contact a relevant organization such as ALCS (for authors) or PLS (for publishers). You could also search the WATCH database (Writers, Artists, and Their Copyright Holders, see http://tyler.hrc.utexas.edu). The information you require is the name and address of the creator.

2 If you can, locate the copyright owner, make contact and request permission to copy (see Figures 9.4 and 9.5).

3 If the creator is truly anonymous, then it is worth putting an advertisement or a letter into a relevant trade journal or national newspaper, asking for the rightsholder to make themselves known to you, or asking if anyone can help you locate the rightsholder. At this point if there is no forthcoming information and the creator is untraceable, then you have to make a judgement as to whether or not to carry on and digitize the item. This is, in effect, a question of assessing the legal risks involved in what you plan to do.

4 If you do go ahead and digitize the item, it is best to annotate the digital copy with a notice stating how you made reasonable efforts to obtain copyright clearance.

5 If the copyright owner comes forward at this stage, bear in mind that you are infringing their rights. However, by using the due diligence files, you can prove that you made reasonable efforts to find the copyright owner.

Library and information professionals are normally keen to ensure that their activities stay on the right side of copyright law. The problem is that obtaining the necessary clearance can be a long-winded and time-consuming

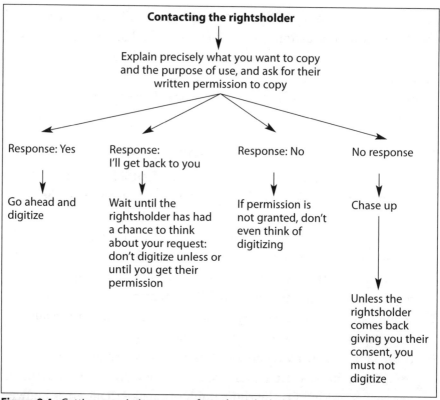

Figure 9.4 Getting permission to copy from the rightsholder

Copyright Release Form: Photographs and Videos

I (name)_____

of (address) _____

_____

- Agree that my photograph/video may be taken/recorded* for possible inclusion in [details of the website/package/VLE]
- Agree that the photograph/video recording may be used with the above context at the discretion of Xyz University.

The resulting website/teaching and learning materials will be used internally by staff and students of Xyz University.

If at a later date commercial exploitation of these materials is considered, then at that point your permission will be sought to include the photograph/video.

NB: Your contribution will not be used without your permission.

Signed _____

Figure 9.5 Copyright release form

Pre-digitization checklist

1 Separate the materials into three categories: self-written, those written by colleagues and those which have third party materials in them. If the self-written materials and those written by colleagues fall under the legal category of having been prepared in the course of employment, then a check should be made with your employer that digitization will be permitted.

2 Are the third party materials licensed by a blanket licence (e.g. CLA, ERA, NLA)? If not, does written permission to copy the materials exist?

3 Does the licensed material allow for change of media – there may be a licence for photocopying materials but does it say anything about digitizing and electronic storage of the materials? The CLA now has various digitization licences available for different business and educational sectors. The terms for digitization vary from licence to licence, so check these carefully. If there are no appropriate terms in the licence, then it is likely that permission will have to be obtained.

4 If you have materials which are not covered by a licence or by written permission, and therefore you have no permission to digitize, permission must be sought from the rightsholders.

5 Can the rightsholders be identified from the materials? Is it easy to contact the rightsholders?

6 If existing digitized material (e.g. CD-ROM) forms part of the materials and is to be further copied by placing on a VLE, for example, it is unlikely that this transfer would be allowed – check the terms and conditions that come with the CD-ROM.

7 Is the material still under a copyright term (70 years after the death of the author or 25 years from the date of publication for the typographical layout of the edition you want to use)?

8 Are there any exceptions you can call upon?

9 If you are unable to digitize because there is no licence and it is difficult to contact the rightsholders, consider directing students to other digital resources – SCRAN, Education Media Online, etc. Check with your library/resource unit to determine which resources they have and which can be accessed by you and your students.

10 Ensure that any materials which can be legitimately digitized are accompanied at all times by an acknowledgement or source.

(This checklist has been reproduced with the kind permission of Alan Rae of Dundee College.)

process, especially when a number of different rights have to be cleared. What librarians often want is a one-stop-shop solution.

The Copyright Clearance Center (CCC), the US reproduction rights organization, has a set of copyright integration services which are designed to allow users to obtain copyright permission both quickly and easily. They do this by enabling libraries to incorporate the clearance process within their software applications, and this results in a streamlined workflow.

The CCC has, for example, partnered with the library management system provider SIRSI Dynix, so that users of their Resolver product have the process of obtaining copyright compliance built into their workflow (www.sirsi.com/Newsevents/Releases/20050405ccc.html). The electronic reserves software Dokutek ERes has also been integrated with the CCC's online permission services.

The CCC has a copyright compliance tool called 'Rightsphere', which is a web-based rights advisory and management service to help corporations promote collaboration and the free flow of published information while also respecting copyright.

One consideration with copyright clearance is whether or not a fee is going to be charged for the copying, and if so at what level the permission fee is set. You need to be clear with the rightsholder precisely what it is that you want permission to do, because this can have a significant bearing on the level of fee to be paid.

9.4 Penalties for infringement

The penalty for a copyright offence currently depends on whether the infringement occurred online or not. For those who deal commercially in infringing goods, or those who distribute goods other than in the course of business to an extent which prejudicially affects the rightsholder, the maximum penalty is ten years' imprisonment. In contrast, those who commit online infringement by communicating the work to the public (whether commercial or otherwise) may be sentenced to up to two years' imprisonment. Finally, the commercial showing or playing in public of a work carries a maximum of six months' imprisonment or a level five fine.

This discrepancy arises following the implementation some years back of the Copyright, etc. and Trade Marks (Offences and Enforcement) Act

Table 9.1 Penalties for infringement

Nature of offence	Communicating to the public by electronic transmission in the course of a business or to an extent prejudicially affecting the rightsowner	Making infringing copies for sale or hire	Distributing infringing copies in the course of business or to an extent that prejudicially affects the rightsholder, importing an infringing copy into the UK other than for private or domestic purposes
Summary sentence (in magistrates' courts)	Up to three months in prison and/or statutory maximum fine	Up to six months in prison and/or statutory maximum fine	Up to six months in prison and/or statutory maximum fine
Sentence on indictment (in Crown Court)	Up to two years in prison and/or unlimited fine	Up to ten years in prison and/or unlimited fine	Up to ten years in prison and/or unlimited fine

Source: Table 5.3 of the Gowers Review

2002. Table 9.1 provides a summary of the current penalties for online and physical copyright infringement.

The Review proposes that the penalty for online commercial infringement should be increased to ten years' imprisonment to bring parity with commercially dealing in pirated works (but not showing them). In addition, it proposes that the penalty for consumers who infringe online to an extent that prejudicially affects the rightsholder should also be extended to ten years, again to bring parity with physical infringement. Recommendation 36 states: 'Match penalties for online and physical copyright infringement by amending section 107 of the CDPA by 2008.'

➡ Relevant legal cases

Lowry's Reports v Legg Mason

Legg Mason shared one paid $700 subscription to Lowry's *Market Trend Analysis* with more than 1,300 employees over the company's intranet. In mid-2003 the federal district court in Maryland found Legg Mason liable to Lowry's for breach of contract and wilful copyright infringement.

Legg Mason was required to pay newsletter publisher Lowry's Reports $19,725,270 in damages and lost subscription fees. Legg Mason went back to court in February 2004 seeking a reduction in the award for damages, but the figure was upheld.

9.5 Copyright ownership

In general, the author of a work is the first owner of any copyright in it.

9.5.1 Work made during course of employment

When a work is made by an employee in the course of his or her employment, then the employer is the first owner of any copyright in the work unless there is a written agreement to the contrary.

This only applies to employees and not to contractors, so the mere fact that a work has been commissioned and paid for does not give ownership of copyright to the commissioning party.

It is important to include a clause in contracts with freelancers or outside companies which deals with the question of ownership of the rights in any content produced. An organization may, for example, wish to publish information on a website or intranet. That information may come from a number of sources: external developers and consultants, internal employees, etc. The organization in question will therefore need to secure in writing the assignment of rights from any third parties, and must also ensure that any employees created the content during the course of their employment.

9.5.2 Commissioned photographs

The CDPA 1988 removed provisions under earlier law whereby the commissioner of the photograph, portrait or engraving was the first owner of copyright. The position now is that a photographer is an author on equal

Tip

It is always in your interest to double-check any contract with a freelance photographer and to make sure that you are acquiring the rights to the photographs.

terms with a journalist. The photographer is therefore the first owner of copyright unless they enter into a written contract to the contrary. If a freelance photographer is paid a fee to take a number of photographs, the photographer will own copyright and in order to acquire copyright ownership, the commissioner of the photograph would need to obtain a letter from the photographer assigning the copyright over. Some freelance photographers do not assign copyright, preferring instead to license the use of commissioned photographs for a specific act. The photographer would then be able to use the photographs again if they are non-personal, even though they have been paid for by a commissioning party.

9.5.3 Transfer of ownership

Copyright may be assigned, like any other property right. In order for the assignment to be valid in law, it must be made in writing and signed by or on behalf of the owner of the copyright, provided the person making the assignment has the necessary authority.

When an author is looking for a suitable publisher to publish their work, they may find that the publisher asks for permission to be cleared for 'all forms and editions', even where a more limited licence would be sufficient. A typical clause in a publisher's contract might be something like:

> The assignment in clause xyz includes the right to publish or adapt the material in the manuscript or any part of it for use in conjunction with computer systems and/or programs including reproduction or publication in machine readable form and/or incorporation in retrieval systems.

If this is to cover possible publication at some future date it is better for the author not to give away all their electronic rights, but instead to say that they will be happy to negotiate with the publisher when they are clear about their plans to publish a digital copy of the work. When that does happen, it is better for the author to agree a licence with the publisher, rather than assigning over all of their electronic rights.

Further information

Society of Authors (2003) *Publishing Contracts: Society of Authors quick guide 8.*

9.6 Crown copyright and re-use of public sector information

OPSI, the UK's Office of Public Sector Information, which forms one part of the National Archives, manages and licenses the re-use of Crown copyright material, defining policy and providing advice and guidance on a range of copyright matters. OPSI also licenses the re-use of parliamentary copyright material on behalf of the Westminster and Scottish Parliaments. In addition, OPSI delegates certain Crown copyright licensing responsibilities to other government departments and agencies, overseeing the administration of those delegated responsibilities and investigating any infringements of Crown and parliamentary copyright.

As an accredited Information Fair Trader, OPSI's licensing team has published a statement on the standards of fairness that they seek to achieve in licensing the re-use of Crown copyright material.

OPSI produces a series of copyright guidance notes (see www.opsi.gov.uk/advice/crown-copyright/copyright-guidance/index.htm). Guidance note number 6, for example, covers reproduction of UK, England, Wales and Northern Ireland primary and secondary legislation.

There is a Crown copyright waiver, but the use of the term 'waiver' here is a little misleading. In this instance, it means that the Crown is not seeking to exercise its legal right to licence formally, restrict usage or charge for the reproduction of the material. However, Crown copyright is asserted to protect the material against use in a misleading or derogatory manner.

Provided that the obligations set out in the guidance note are complied with, there are no restrictions on how the material may be reproduced. By way of illustration, users may undertake any of the following activities:

- reproduce and publish the material in any medium
- reproduce the material on free and subscription websites which are accessible via the internet

- establish hypertext links to the official legislation websites which feature the complete text of current legislation, with accompanying 'Explanatory Notes for Acts'
- download and print the material featured on the legislation websites
- reproduce the material on intranet sites.

The user's obligations include the following:

- All reproduction of the material should be made from an official version.
- The material must be reproduced accurately.
- Care should be taken that the material reproduced is from the current or up to date version, and that out of date material is not presented as though it was current.
- The material should not be used in a derogatory or misleading manner, nor should it be used for the purposes of advertising or promoting a particular product or service or for promoting particular personal interests or views.
- The reproduced version of material should not be presented in a way which could imply it has official status or is endorsed by any part of government.
- All publisher imprints which are featured on the official versions of the material should be removed from any copies of the material which are issued or made available to the public.
- Royal Arms may only be reproduced when they form an integral part of the material being reproduced and are used in that context.
- The material must be acknowledged appropriately.

The Parliamentary Copyright (National Assembly for Wales) Order 2007: SI 2007/1116 modifies the provisions of Section 165 of the Copyright, Designs and Patents Act 1988 (Parliamentary copyright) so that its provisions apply with modifications to works made by or under the direction or control of the National Assembly of Wales. By virtue of Subsection (7) of Section 165 of the CDPA 1988, the provisions of that section apply not only in respect of works made by or under the direction or control of the

House of Commons or the House of Lords, but also, subject to any exceptions or modifications specified by Order in Council, to works made by or under the direction or control of any other legislative body of a country to which Part I of the Act extends. Part I of the Act extends to Wales. By virtue of Part III of the Government of Wales Act 2006, the National Assembly of Wales has legislative powers.

The National Assembly for Wales Commission is the first owner of any copyright in works made by or under the direction or control of the National Assembly for Wales. In addition, works made in the course of their duties by the Presiding Officer and the Deputy Presiding Officer of the National Assembly for Wales, by members of the National Assembly for Wales Commission and by members of the staff of the Assembly are works made by or under the direction or control of the National Assembly of Wales for the purposes of Section 165.

Schedules 10 and 12 of the Government of Wales Act 2006 remove Crown copyright (Section 163: First owner: HM the Queen) from works produced by the National Assembly for Wales, because the Assembly is not a Crown body. Instead, the Assembly owns the copyright itself and is allowed to decide what to do with it, as is also the case with the Scottish Parliament and the Northern Ireland Assembly. The term of protection is 50 years.

On 1 July 2005 the Re-use of Public Sector Information Regulations came into force. These introduced a scheme regulating the re-use of public sector information. The main obligations under the Regulations are:

- Public sector documents that are available for re-use should be readily identifiable.
- Documents should generally be available for re-use at marginal cost.
- Public sector bodies should deal with applications to re-use in a timely, open and transparent manner.
- The process should be fair, consistent and non-discriminatory.
- The sharing of best practice should be encouraged across the public sector.

The Regulations implemented European Directive 2003/98/EC on the re-use of public sector information. The scheme is overseen by the Office of Public Sector Information. Some public sector bodies are not covered by the directive. These include:

- public service broadcasters
- educational and research establishments
- cultural establishments (including museums, libraries and archives).

There is also an Advisory Panel on Public Sector Information (APPSI) (www.appsi.gov.uk). It is a non-departmental public body, established in April 2003, whose role is:

- to advise Ministers on how to encourage and create opportunities in the information industry for greater re-use of government information
- to advise the Controller of HMSO about changes and opportunities in the information industry, so that the licensing of Crown copyright information is aligned with current and emerging developments
- to advise on the impact of the complaints procedures under the Information Fair Trader Scheme.

In December 2006 the Office of Fair Trading published the findings of a study into the commercial use of public sector information (PSI). The study looked at the markets for PSI and how well the supply of PSI was working for customers, particularly:

- what PSI is made available for re-use, at what price and on what terms
- whether businesses can compete with PSI holders in the supply of products/services to which value has been added.

The OFT concluded that improvements should be made, and that these improvements should preferably be achieved without legislation. Given the potential importance of the sector to the economy, the OFT proposed evaluating the impact of the recommendations made in their report after two to three years. If, at this stage, the recommendations are not taking effect among PSI holders, the OFT has said that it will consider again the case for further action, including the possibility of increasing the regulatory powers affecting the sector.

Further information

Cabinet Office (2007) *The Government's Response to the Power of Information: an independent review by Ed Mayo and Tom Steinberg,* www.cabinetoffice.gov.uk/publications/reports/power_information/power_information_response.pdf.

Office of Fair Trading (2006) *The Commercial Use of Public Information*, OFT.

Notes

1   The list of excluded works at www.cla.co.uk/support/excluded.html sets out a list of countries whose content is covered by the CLA licences. Any works published outside these countries would not be covered by the CLA licences.

2   In the case of the Isle of Man, copyright is protected under the Copyright Act 1991 (an Act of Tynwald) generally for 50 years after the death of the author (not 70 years as in member states of the EU). However, database right does extend to the Isle of Man, courtesy of the Copyright and Rights in Databases (Amendment) Regulations 2003: SI 2003/2501.

The Bailiwick of Guernsey, comprising the Island of Guernsey (with the adjacent islets of Herm and Jethou), Alderney and Sark, is a self-governing Crown Dependency with its own legislative assembly and systems of law and administration, including intellectual property laws. For further information, see www.ipo.gov.uk/guernsey.pdf and www.gov.gg/ipo.

The Bailiwick of Jersey is a self-governing Crown Dependency with its own legislative assembly and systems of law and administration, including intellectual property laws.

10

Useful resources

10.1 List of useful addresses

British Universities Film and Video Council

77 Wells Street
London W1T 3QJ
Tel: 020 7393 1500
Fax: 020 7393 1555
www.bufvc.ac.uk

CILIP (for copyright posters)

7 Ridgmount Street
London WC1E 7AE
Tel: 020 7255 0500
www.cilip.org.uk/professionalguidance/copyright/
formsandposters/posters.htm

Copyright Licensing Agency

Saffron House
6–10 Kirby Street
London EC1N 8TS
Tel: 020 7400 3100
Fax: 020 7400 3101
www.cla.co.uk

Design and Artists Copyright Society

33 Great Sutton Street
London EC1V 0DX
Tel: 020 7336 8811
Fax: 020 7336 8822
www.dacs.co.uk

EBLIDA

PO Box 16359
NL-2500 BJ The Hague
The Netherlands
Tel: +31 70 309 0551
Fax: +31 70 309 0558
E-mail: eblida@debibliotheken.nl
www.eblida.org

Educational Recording Agency

New Premier House
150 Southampton Row
London WC1B 5AL
Tel: 020 7837 3222
Fax: 020 7837 3750
E-mail: era@era.org.uk
www.era.org.uk

HERON, a division of Ingenta

Unipart House
Garsington Road
Oxford OX4 2GQ
Tel: 01865 397800
Fax: 01865 397801
www.heron.ingenta.com/

JISC Legal Information Service

Learning Services
University of Strathclyde
Alexander Turnbull Building
155 George Street
Glasgow G1 1RD
Tel: 0141 548 4939
Fax: 0141 548 4216
E-mail: info@jisclegal.ac.uk
www.jisclegal.ac.uk

Newspaper Licensing Agency

7–9 Church Road
Wellington Gate
Tunbridge Wells TN1 1NL
Tel: 01892 525273
Fax: 01892 525275
E-mail: copy@nla.co.uk
www.nla.co.uk

Office of Public Sector Information

www.opsi.gov.uk
www.opsi.gov.uk/about/contact-us/index.htm

RNIB

105 Judd Street
London WC1H 9NE
Tel: 020 7388 1266
Fax: 020 7388 2034
Helpline: 0845 766 9999
www.rnib.org.uk

Technical Advisory Service for Images

Institute for Learning and Research Technology
University of Bristol
8–10 Berkeley Square
Bristol BS8 1HH
Tel: 0117 928 7091
E-mail: info@tasi.ac.uk
www.tasi.ac.uk

UK Intellectual Property Office

Enquiry line: 0845 9 500 505
E-mail: copyright@ipo.gov.uk
www.ipo.gov.uk

10.2 Keeping up to date

CILIP – daily news bulletin

www.cilip.org.uk/enquiryandsearch/newsbulletin/default.htm
The daily news bulletin regularly includes items on copyright and other
intellectual property rights and plagiarism. It is a service for CILIP
members only.

Digital Media Law Update

Produced by Glyn Morgan of Taylor Wessing.
E-mail: g.morgan@taylorwessing.com

EDRI: Digital Civil Rights in Europe

EDRI/Copyright: www.edri.org/issues/copyright
EDRI-gram: www.edri.org/edrigram

EUROPA Copyright and Neighbouring Rights News

http://europa.eu.int/comm/internal_market/copyright/news/news_en.htm

IP Kat

http://ipkitten.blogspot.com/atom.xml (RSS feed)

IPR Helpdesk

www.ipr-helpdesk.org/index.htm
RSS newsfeed: www.ipr-helpdesk.org/rss?ver=10&len=en

JISC Legal Information Service news

www.jisclegal.ac.uk/news.htm

LIB-LICENSE (licensing digital information: a resource for librarians)

www.library.yale.edu/~llicense/index.shtml

LIS-Copyseek

www.jiscmail.ac.uk/lists/lis-copyseek.html
Closed discussion list for copyright permission seekers.
E-mail address to contact the list owners:
lis-copyseek-request@jiscmail.ac.uk

Mondaq

www.mondaq.com

It is possible to register to receive tailored e-mail alerts covering topics such as copyright or licensing and syndication.

NLA eClips blog
http://eclips.squarespace.com/blog/atom.xml

Out-law.com: copyright RSS feed
www.out-law.com/feeds/out-law_copyright.aspx

The TASI lightbox
www.tasi.ac.uk/blog/?feed=rss2

10.3 Legislation
10.3.1 International

Berne Convention for the Protection of Literary and Artistic Works 1886
    www.wipo.int/treaties/en/ip/berne/trtdocs_wo001.html
Universal Copyright Convention
    www.unesco.org/culture/laws/copyright/html_eng/page1.shtml
Universal Declaration of Human Rights
    www.un.org/Overview/rights.html
WIPO Copyright Treaty 1996
    www.wipo.int/documents/en/diplconf/distrib/94dc.htm

10.3.2 European

Directive 96/9/EC of the European Parliament and of the Council of 11
    March 1996 on the legal protection of databases
    http://europa.eu.int/smartapi/cgi/sga_doc?smartapi!celexapi!prod!
    celexnumdoc&lg=en&numdoc=31996L0009&model=guichett
Directive 1999/93/EC of the European Parliament and of the Council of 13
    December 1999 on a community framework for electronic signatures

http://europa.eu.int/eur-lex/pri/en/oj/dat/
2000/l_013/l_01320000119en00120020.pdf

Directive 2001/29/EC of the European Parliament and of the Council of 22
May 2001 on the harmonization of certain aspects of copyright and
related rights in the information society
http://europa.eu.int/smartapi/cgi/sga_doc?smartapi!celexapi!prod!
celexnumdoc&lg=en&numdoc=32001L0029&model=guichett

Directive 2003/98/EC of the European Parliament and of the Council on the
re-use of public sector information
http://europa.eu.int/eur-lex/pri/en/oj/dat/2003/
l_345/l_34520031231en00900096.pdf

Directive 2004/48/EC of the European Parliament and of the Council of 29
April 2004 on the enforcement of intellectual property rights
http://europa.eu.int/eur-lex/pri/en/oj/dat/2004/l_195/
l_19520040602en00160025.pdf

Directive 2006/115/EC of the European Parliament and of the Council of 12
December 2006 on rental right and lending right and on certain rights
related to copyright in the field of intellectual property (codified version)
(replaces Directive 92/100/EEC)
http://eur-lex.europa.eu/lexuriserv/
lexuriserv.do?uri=celex:32006l0115:en:not

Directive 2006/116/EC of the European Parliament and of the Council of 12
December 2006 on the term of protection of copyright and certain related
rights (codified version) (replaces Directive 93/98/EEC)
http://eur-lex.europa.eu/lexuriserv/
lexuriserv.do?uri=celex:32006l0116:en:not

10.3.3 UK
Acts of Parliament

Copyright, Designs and Patents Act 1988
Copyright (Visually Impaired Persons) Act 2002
www.opsi.gov.uk/acts/acts2002/20020033.htm
Electronic Communications Act 2000
www.opsi.gov.uk/acts/acts2000/20000007.htm

Legal Deposit Libraries Act 2003
  www.opsi.gov.uk/acts/acts2003/20030028.htm
Patents Act 1977
Unfair Contract Terms Act 1977

Statutory instruments

The Copyright and Performances (Application to Other Countries) Order
  2007: SI 2007/273
  www.opsi.gov.uk/si/si2007/20070273.htm
The Copyright and Related Rights Regulations 1996: SI 1996/2967
  www.opsi.gov.uk/si/si1996/uksi_19962967_en_1.htm
The Copyright and Related Rights Regulations 2003: SI 2003/2498
  www.opsi.gov.uk/si/si2003/20032498.htm
The Copyright and Rights in Databases Regulations 1997: SI 1997/3032
  www.opsi.gov.uk/si/si1997/19973032.htm
The Copyright and Rights in Databases (Amendment) Regulations 2003:
  SI 2003/2501
The Copyright (Certification of Licensing Scheme for Educational Recording
  of Broadcasts) (Educational Recording Agency Limited) Order 2007:
  SI 2007/266
  www.opsi.gov.uk/si/si2007/20070266.htm
The Copyright (Educational Establishments) Order 2005: SI 2005/223
  www.opsi.gov.uk/si/si2005/20050223.htm
The Copyright (Librarians and Archivists) (Copying of Copyright Material)
  Regulations 1989: SI 1989/1212
  www.opsi.gov.uk/si/si1989/uksi_19891212_en_1.htm
The Electronic Signatures Regulations 2002: SI 2002/318
  www.opsi.gov.uk/si/si2002/20020318.htm
The Parliamentary Copyright (National Assembly for Wales) Order 2007:
  SI 2007/1116
  www.opsi.gov.uk/si/si2007/uksi_20071116_en.pdf
The Re-use of Public Sector Information Regulations 2005: SI 2005/1515
  www.opsi.gov.uk/si/si2005/20051515.htm
The Unfair Terms in Consumer Contracts Regulations 1999: SI 1999/2083
  www.opsi.gov.uk/si/si1999/19992083.htm

Note

The legislation available through the OPSI website (www.opsi.gov.uk/legislation/about_legislation.htm) does not include any subsequent modifications. You will therefore need to consult an annotated copy of the legislation. For example:

■ Blackstone's Statutes on Intellectual Property
■ Butterworths Intellectual Property Law Handbook.

In March 2005, the UK Intellectual Property Office made available on its website an unofficial consolidated text of UK legislation to 31 December 2003. This can be found at www.ipo.gov.uk/cdpact1988.pdf.

The UK Statute Law Database can be found at www.statutelaw.gov.uk – this is the official revised edition of the primary legislation of the UK (although not as yet fully up to date).

10.4 Further information and additional resources

All Party Internet Group (2006) *All Party Internet Group Report into Digital Rights Management*,
www.apcomms.org.uk/apig/current-activities/apig-inquiry-into-digital-rights-management.html.

Bultmann, B. et al. (2005) *Digitised Content in the UK Research Library and Archives Sector*, JISC.

Burrell, Robert and Coleman, Alison (2005) *Copyright Exceptions: the digital impact*, Cambridge Studies in Intellectual Property Rights, Cambridge University Press.

Casey, John (2006) *Intellectual Property Rights in Networked e-Learning*, JISC Legal.

Charman, Suw (2006) *Copyright in a Collaborative Age*, M/C Journal, 9.2.

Committee for Economic Development (2004) *Promoting Innovation and Economic Growth: the special problem of digital IP*,
www.ced.org.

Congress of the United States, Congressional Budget Office (2004) *Copyright Issues in Digital Media*,
www.cbo.gov/showdoc.cfm?index=5738&sequence=0.

Davies, William (2005) *Markets in the Online Public Sphere*, IPPR.

Davies, William (2005) *Modernising with Purpose: a manifesto for a digital Britain*, Institute for Public Policy Research.

Davis, Randall (2000) *The Digital Dilemma*, National Academic Press, http://books.nap.edu/catalog/9601.html?onpi_newsdoc110399.

Department of Trade and Industry/Publishers Association (2002) *Combating Internet Copyright Crime*, DTI/PA.

Durrant, Fiona (2006) *Negotiating Licences for Digital Resources*, Facet Publishing.

Electronic Information for Libraries (2007) *eIFL-IP Handbook on Copyright and Related Issues for Libraries*, www.eifl.net/cps/sections/services/eifl-ip/issues/eifl-handbook-on.

EU's High Level Expert Group on Digital Libraries (2007) *Model Agreement for a Licence on Digitization of Out of Print Works*, http://ec.europa.eu/information_society/newsroom/cf/ itemlongdetail.cfm?item_id=3366.

EU's High Level Expert Group on Digital Libraries (2007) *Report on Digital Preservation, Orphan Works and Out-of-Print Works: selected implementation issues*, http://ec.europa.eu/information_society/newsroom/cf/ itemlongdetail.cfm?item_id=3366.

Frankel, Mark (2002) *Seizing the Moment: scientists' authorship rights in the digital age*, American Association for the Advancement of Science.

Gartner2 and the Berkman Center for Internet and Society (2003) *Copyright and Digital Media in a Post Napster World*, Gartner2, http://cyber.law.harvard.edu/home/uploads/254/2003-05.pdf.

Institute for Information Law (1998) *Privacy, Data Protection and Copyright: their interaction in the context of electronic copyright management systems*, Institute for Information Law.

International Federation of Library Associations and Institutions (2002) *Limitations and Exceptions to Copyright and Neighbouring Rights in the Digital Environment*, IFLA.

IPR Helpdesk (n.d.) *Copyright and Internet Guide*, IPR Helpdesk.

IPR Helpdesk (n.d.) *Creating a Website*, IPR Helpdesk.

IPR Helpdesk (2005) *Intellectual Property Aspects of World Wide Web Authoring*, IPR Helpdesk.

Jeweler, Robin (2007) *Internet Search Engines: copyright's 'fair use' in reproduction and public display rights*, Congressional Research Service.

Lessig, Lawrence (2006) *Code (Version 2.0)*, Perseus Books.

Litman, Jessica (2001) *Digital Copyright*, Prometheus Books.

MacQueen, Hector (2006) *UK Copyright Law in the Digital Environment*, Netherlands Comparative Law Association.

Morrison, Alex (2004) *Briefing Paper on Copyright in Screenshots*, JISC Legal.

Murphy, Anthony (2002) *Queen Anne and the Anarchists: can copyright survive in the electronic age*, Oxford Intellectual Property Research Centre.

Museum Documentation Association (2003) *Digital Copyright* (MDA copyright factsheet), www.mda.org.uk/cdigi.htm.

Pedley, Paul (2005) Is Digital Content Treated Differently in Law?, *Library & Information Update*, (October).

Pedley, Paul (ed.) (2005) *Managing Digital Rights: a practitioner's guide*, Facet Publishing.

Publishers Association (1998) *Copyright in the Digital Age*, www.publishers.org.uk/paweb/paweb.nsf/homepages/ guidelines+(public)!opendocument.

Publishers Association (1999) *Copyright Licensing in an Electronic Environment* www.publishers.org.uk/paweb/paweb.nsf/homepages/ guidelines+(public)!opendocument.

Publishers Association (1999) *Use of Digitised Copyright Works in Libraries*, www.publishers.org.uk/paweb/paweb.nsf/homepages/ guidelines+(public)!opendocument.

Shapiro, Michael (n.d.) *Museums and the Digital Future*, International Intellectual Property Institute.

Story, Alan (2002) *Study on Intellectual Property Rights, the Internet and Copyright*, www.iprcommission.org/papers/word/study_papers/sp5_story_study.doc.

Sutter, Gavin and Gibson, Johanna (2007) *Podcasts and the Law*, JISC Legal.

Vaknin, Sam (2005) Free Public Domain and Copyrighted Ebooks Online, http://www.freepint.com/issues/140705.htm#tips.

Various (2006) *Copyright and E-learning Webcast*, JISC Legal.

WIPO (2002) *Intellectual Property on the Internet: a survey of issues*, WIPO.

Index

KWtL — Keeping Within the Law

Keeping Within the Law
Legal issues for information users, suppliers and providers

KWtL's editor Paul Pedley is Head of Research at The Economist Intelligence Unit. KWtL encapsulates his extensive experience in the copyright and information rights field to create one comprehensive source of advice, guidance and information for whoever advises people in the organization on what can and cannot be done in relation to copyright and information law issues. KWtL is the only product of its kind. Make sure you don't miss out on this remarkable opportunity to stay informed about protecting and respecting intellectual property rights in the most challenging area of information practice by subscribing to KWtL.

KWtL is an annual subscription product consisting of an evolving databank of resources, a subscribers-only daily blog, news, premium content in-depth reports and a monthly newsletter covering legal issues for the information stakeholder community: information suppliers, professionals and providers. It will highlight the complex legal issues affecting these communities, flag up legal risks and offer solutions as to how those risks can be managed and minimized.

KWtL aims to raise awareness of the legal issues faced by information professionals in their work. Subscribers have access to content which highlights areas of potential risk, and practical ways in which people can reduce those risks are outlined. This content is updated regularly, and new content on areas of interest will be added throughout the subscription year.

more...

Exclusive advantages of subscribing to KWtL

- 12 issues of the KWtL e-newsletter
- exclusive, password-protected access to the regularly updated KWtL website with fully searchable access to its resources and archive
- full access to in-depth news stories and the editor's web picks
- 25% discount on all Facet Publishing books on copyright and information rights
- discounts on selected CILIP Enterprise executive briefings and training courses

Visit Paul's blog (http://informationlaw.blogspot.com) for comments and news before the launch date.

How to subscribe

Annual subscription £225.00 (CILIP Members' discount does not apply.) Available direct from Facet Publishing, this product is available on an individual subscriber basis only. Full information on how to subscribe will be available when the site launches in Autumn 2007. However, if you have any queries in the meantime, please contact the Sales Department on 0207 255 0594 or e-mail info@facetpublishing.co.uk.

Keeping
Within
the Law